No Hype

The Straight Goods
on Investing Your Money

Gail Bebee

THE
GANNETH
COMPANY

Library and Archives Canada Cataloguing in Publication

Bebee, Gail, 1951–
    No hype–the straight goods on investing your money / Gail Bebee.

Includes index.
ISBN 978-0-9784455-0-8

1. Investments.   2. Finance, Personal. I. Title.

HG4521.B4241 2008   332.67'8   C2007-905462-5

Published by
The Ganneth Company
17 Blithfield Avenue
Toronto, Ontario M2K 1X9
Canada

Visit us online at **www.nohypeinvesting.com**

Editing: Catherine Leek, Green Onion Publishing
Design and Print Production: Heidy Lawrance, WeMakeBooks.ca
Printed and bound in Canada

To the late Arthur Steuermann,
a friend and mentor whose investing wisdom
is a continuing inspiration.

Acknowledgements

I owe thanks to many people who helped turn my dream of writing a book on investing into reality. First, I owe a depth of gratitude to my family who good naturedly endured my unrelenting preoccupation with writing this book over the past year and supported my efforts. My husband, Ken Kurkowski, encouraged me to pursue my dream and provided thoughtful and constructive input throughout the creation of this book. My son, Jeff, provided key input during my search for the perfect title to describe the book.

My sincere thanks go to Peter Petropoulos, Bert Barrow, Phyllis Barrow, Claire Pageau, Anne Mirgalet-Kennedy, Jennifer Young, David Trahair and Carolyn Watson who all volunteered to read and comment on drafts of the book while it was still a work in progress. I am grateful to Noel Shippey for his help with the math section of the book. The excellent feedback these wonderful friends provided significantly improved the final product.

While writing this book, I had conversations with many friends and acquaintances about a wide range of investing issues. I thank all these people for their ideas and opinions which influenced my thinking and contributed to a better book.

Writing a book is one thing, selling is quite another. Thanks go to Susan Antler and Lisa Stonehouse for their invaluable assistance with the marketing end of this project.

I am grateful to Catherine Leek who professionally and ably edited the manuscript of an amateur. I must also thank Heidy Lawrance and her associates whose guidance throughout the entire process of morphing a word processing document into a beautiful printed product was exceptional.

Table of Contents

Legal Disclaimer

I wrote this book to provide readers with my opinions and ideas in regard to investing. The book is intended as a general guide only and should not be considered the ultimate source for any of the information contained herein. Any examples provided in this book are for illustrative purposes only and are not a recommendation to buy or sell or an indication of what rate of return or future amount of money you might have if you follow the specific examples. In the interest of full disclosure, readers are advised that I, Gail Bebee, may own some of the investments used as examples for illustrative purposes.

I am not a professional with regard to any of the information contained in this book. The publisher and I are not engaged in rendering legal, accounting, investing, taxation, realty or other professional advice or services in this publication. Readers must undertake further research and must seek the advice of a qualified professional before taking any action related to the information in this book.

This publication may contain errors or omissions. The information contained in this book has been obtained from sources which we believe are reliable. However, we cannot guarantee the completeness or accuracy of the contents. The author and publisher would welcome any further information pertaining to any errors or omissions in order to make corrections in subsequent editions.

The author, Gail Bebee, the publisher, The Ganneth Company, and other persons involved in the creation of this publication expressly disclaim any responsibility for any liability, loss, risk, damage or perceived damage, personal or otherwise, that is caused or alleged to have been caused, directly or indirectly, as a consequence of the use and application of any of the contents of this book. By reading this book, you fully accept these conditions.

Abbreviations

ADR	American Depositary Receipt
AMEX	American Stock Exchange
CDIC	Canada Deposit Insurance Corporation
CSB	Canada Savings Bond
CRA	Canada Revenue Agency
CPI	Consumer Price Index
DJIA	Dow Jones Industrial Average
DRIP	Dividend Reinvestment Savings Plan
DSC	Deferred Sales Charge
ETF	Exchange-Traded Fund
GICs	Guaranteed Investment Certificate
LIRA	Locked-in Retirement Account
LRRSP	Locked-in Registered Retirement Savings Plan
LSIF	Labour Sponsored Investment Fund
MER	Management Expense Ratio
MIC	Mortgage Investment Corporation
NASDAQ	National Association of Securities Dealers Automated Quotations System
NAV	Net Asset Value
NYSE	New York Stock Exchange
RESP	Registered Education Savings Plan
REIT	Real Estate Investment Trust
RRSP	Registered Retirement Savings Plan
SPP	Share Purchase Plans
SEDAR	System for Electronic Document Analysis and Retrieval
S & P	Standards and Poor's
TSX	Toronto Stock Exchange

Part I

The Basics

1

Why Another
Investment Book?
-My Story

An investment in knowledge pays the best interest.

Benjamin Franklin

Many would question whether the world needs another book on investing. So, by way of answering this very valid query, I'll begin with the story of why I wrote *No Hype—The Straight Goods on Investing Your Money*, how it is different from the vast number of other books on investing and why you must read this book.

One day when I was in my mid-40s, after reading an article about how there won't be enough money in the Canada Pension Plan to pay for baby boomer pensions, I realized that at some point in the foreseeable future I would retire from the working world and need an ongoing retirement income. At that point, I took a close look at our family's savings, potential company pension benefits and government old age pension benefits. With the help of a financial planner, our family estimated how much money we would need to retire.

Like many other Canadians, every year my husband and I faithfully contributed to our Registered Retirement Savings Plans (RRSPs). This usually occurred during the annual RRSP marketing frenzy when our stockbroker called to remind us to contribute before the end of February to ensure we benefitted from the tax deduction. We then promptly forgot about our RRSPs and regular investing accounts unless the broker called. If we had spare money, we would buy a Canada Savings Bond (CSB) or whatever investment our broker recommended.

I had no idea what kind of investment return our savings had delivered over the years. I wasn't even sure why I had purchased many of the investments I owned. They were all recommendations made by my broker.

When I examined the individual investments inside our accounts, I found that we mainly owned mutual funds. So, I began to educate myself about mutual funds. I read the fund literature periodically sent by our broker and I perused the fund returns published in the newspaper. (This was before the era of online access to such information). What I found was disturbing. The main fund in my locked-in RRSP account was heavily invested in stocks of Latin American countries. At the time, such stocks were considered high risk, certainly not the best choice for a retirement account. I also discovered that our funds were not the top performers and had relatively high management expense fees compared to other funds of the same type. With a little digging, I found out why. Our funds were the best investment for our broker, not necessarily for us. The companies selling these funds provided the best sales commissions and ongoing fees to brokers.

With this new-found knowledge, I asked my broker to buy two funds that had performed well over the past several years. She did not encourage me to buy these funds. I eventually figured out why – these funds did not pay hefty sales commissions. Moreover, these funds did not pay ongoing fees to brokers to encourage them to keep their clients in the funds.

> I realized that our family needed to take ownership of our investments.

This incident was a wake up call.

I realized that our family needed to take ownership of our investments. We needed to make our own informed decisions about how to best invest our hard earned money.

And so my journey in search of how to invest successfully began.

I started to read the business section of our daily newspaper. I devoured books on investing. I searched for investing magazines at local bookstores. During my lunch hour, I frequented the library near my office and read the latest issues of the investing periodicals found in the reference section. Eventually, I even subscribed to some of them. I tuned into business television and became a regular viewer of such shows as *Market Call* and *Moneyline*. I surfed the Internet in search of the latest financial news and views.

Early in my investing education, during one of my periodic forays past the magazine rack at our local bookstore, I noticed a magazine called *Canadian Moneysaver*. Wow! I thought. Canadian content, that's unique. Most of the books and magazines I'd seen on investing were American. The article titles seemed interesting, so I bought a copy.

A few pages inside the cover I read that *Canadian Moneysaver* sponsored ShareClubs, groups of like-minded members who get together to share financial information. This seemed like a good idea, so I attended a local ShareClub meeting. I found members eager to share their investing knowledge with a rookie and ready to learn more. My ShareClub membership has proved to be an invaluable part of my investing education.

As my knowledge increased, I realized that I should consider moving out of mutual funds and investing directly in stocks. To fully understand how stock investing worked, I enrolled in the Canadian Securities Course, one of the basic requirements to be a stockbroker. This was a challenging evening assignment after working all day at my regular job. However, I put in the study hours and completed the course with honours.

With newly discovered confidence, I plunged into the world of stock investing. I resolved to do my own investment research and make my own investment decisions. I opened a discount brokerage account to eliminate the cost of the financial advisor I decided I no longer needed. I made my share of mistakes learning to buy and sell investments online. I bought some stocks and mutual funds that turned an excellent profit and others that were dogs. Over time, I gained a decent understanding of the art of investing and honed a straightforward approach to what it takes to invest successfully.

After retiring from corporate life, I had time to reflect on my investing career. What struck me was the amount of time I spent digging up basic, understandable, non-partisan information on areas of investing I wanted to know about. I realized there was a genuine need for a comprehensive primer on investing written for

No Hype –The
Straight Goods on
Investing Your
Money is the book I
couldn't find when I
began to seriously
focus on investing.

individual Canadians by a non-biased author. So, I set out to fill this gap.

No Hype – The Straight Goods on Investing Your Money is the book I couldn't find when I began to seriously focus on investing. It is a distillation of the knowledge and experience I gained from my years in the investment trenches. It is a book for individual Canadian investors from the pen of an investment industry outsider with nothing to gain by promoting certain financial products or services.

Read *No Hype – The Straight Goods on Investing Your Money* from cover to cover for a broad overview on investing or taste it in small bites for information on a specific topic. In either case, you'll benefit from my school of hard knocks investing experience. You'll become acquainted with investing traps to avoid and find out how to save money on financial fees that eat into your profits. You'll learn about a simple, low cost approach to investing. You'll get the knowledge you need to cut through investment industry hype and profitably invest your heard-earned money.

2

Where to Begin
Your Investing Journey

*It is always wise to look ahead, but difficult to look
further than you can see.*

Sir Winston Churchill

Based on everything I've learned about investing, I believe that
before investing a penny of your hard-earned money, you need to
take stock of how you feel about investing, your current financial
situation and your future plans and goals. Begin this necessary
exercise by asking yourself a number of questions.

- Why do I want to invest? What are my investing needs and
  goals?
- What are my timelines for achieving these goals?
- What is my current financial situation? What are my debts?
  What savings do I have? How much can I afford to invest?
- Will I need ready access to the money I have invested?
- What is my risk tolerance; how much money am I willing to
  lose on an investment?
- How much time am I willing to devote to investing?

It takes time and knowledge to figure out the answers to these
questions. I'll return to them toward the end of this book in the
chapter on creating a personal investment plan – a written summary of your investing goals and how you plan to achieve them.
Do keep these questions in mind as your investing journey unfolds.

Early on, you must embrace what I believe are the two most fundamental steps to investment success.

1. *Pay Off Debt First.* The first investment you should make is to pay off any money you have borrowed. Reducing debt has a guaranteed investment return. It's like receiving a guaranteed rate of return equivalent to the interest rate on your borrowed money. For example, if your credit card charges 18%, a typical interest rate for Canadian credit cards, paying off your balance before interest charges kick in is like receiving an 18% return on your money. You would be hard pressed to earn anything near this return rate on any other investment.

2. *Pay Yourself Before You Spend.* Automatically saving a portion of every dollar you earn is a painless way to build up savings for investing. Many of us have the habit of spending whatever we earn. Consider such a savings plan as spending on yourself first.

   Pay yourself first by arranging for the automatic transfer of a portion of every pay from the bank account where your pay is deposited to a separate savings account. If your employer has an employee savings plan, sign up for automatic contributions from every pay cheque.

Assessing your personal approach to investing, creating plans to pay off debt and paying yourself first are the essential first steps to investing your money profitably. The next stop on your journey is the five universal rules of investing.

3

Five Universal Rules of Investing

He who knows others is wise; he who knows himself is enlightened.

Lao-tzu

To my mind, five universal rules underpin success in any type of investing.

1. Think for yourself.
2. Know yourself.
3. Manage your risk.
4. Be patient.
5. Be decisive.

I'll look at each of these in turn.

1. Think for Yourself

In today's world, there is a mind-boggling cornucopia of information available on investing. Entire television channels are dedicated to the subject (Business News Network, MSNBC, etc.). Most newspapers have a business section that reports on investing related news. The average bookstore carries several shelves of books on investing. There are countless web sites dealing with this topic. And, of course, there is your investment advisor calling periodically to offer new ideas and advice. Even your friend or neighbour may have a tip on the latest hot stock to buy.

Unfortunately, much of this information is not particularly objective. The purveyor of the information often has a hidden agenda or a vested interest in the information being perceived in a way that would be beneficial to him/her personally. Witness these real life examples.

- The CEO being interviewed on business television wants to convince you to buy stock in his company.
- The stockbroker recommending a newly listed stock has been told to promote the stock to reduce his/her company's inventory of the stock.
- The financial advisor steering you toward a certain brand of mutual funds receives a bonus for reaching certain sales targets for these funds.
- The manager of a precious metals mutual fund reports that the outlook for gold is "extremely positive" because he/she wants you to buy this fund.

If there is one thing you take away from this book, it must be this, the number one rule of investing:

Think for yourself before you
make a decision on any investment.

The number one rule of investing: Think for yourself before you make a decision on any investment.

Thinking for yourself means critically appraising any information regarding a potential investment decision and using only the information that passes your scrutiny.

Here are some points to consider as you sift through the reams of investing information you encounter.

- Is the source reliable?
- Is the information current?
- What benefit will the person giving the information receive if I buy an investment he/she recommends?
- What is my own conclusion based on the actual information compared to what the author has concluded?

Don't rely only on the information in news items or analysts' reports; consult original documents and reports.

2. Know Yourself

Each of the over six billion individuals in the world possesses a unique set of character traits. This means that each of us has a unique approach to handling the challenges of life and, it logically follows, the challenges of investing.

In order to invest successfully, you need to be aware of your own unique character strengths and weaknesses and factor these into your investment plans. You need to know yourself. Some specific examples will help you better understand my second universal rule of investing: Know yourself.

> Risk and reward are two concepts that are inextricably linked in the world of investing.

- You make a New Year's resolution to learn how to invest money so you can make all your own investment decisions. However, you have the habit of enthusiastically embracing a new project and then abandoning it when something more interesting crosses your path. So, if you practise the Know Yourself rule, you follow through on your resolution and learn how to invest before firing your financial advisor.
- You plan to buy a small gold mining stock listed on the Canadian Venture Exchange because a co-worker says that his uncle who is a geologist swears that the stock price will double in two months. However, you cannot sleep at night if you lose money on an investment. So, if you practise the Know Yourself rule, you do not buy the high-risk stock, you keep your money in a less risky investment like a government bond or a high quality stock.

3. Manage Your Risk

Risk and reward are two concepts that are inextricably linked in the world of investing. Risk is all about the possibility of suffering a loss. Reward is all about profit. Normally, risk and reward are directly correlated, that is, the riskier the investment, the greater the potential profit.

To invest successfully, every time you think about purchasing an investment you need to manage your investment risk by:

- understanding the chance that the investment will fail (risk) and the profit potential of the investment (reward);
- considering how the specific investment will affect the risk/reward profile of your overall investment portfolio, i.e., all the investments you own; and
- making the purchase decision based on the risk you are willing to assume in your overall portfolio.

At the beginning of your investing career, you will make mistakes. Manage this risk by investing a little and learning from your errors.

4. Be Patient

Work hard, play hard, study hard. It seems that life in today's world is all about living to the max. With so much to do and only 24 hours in the day (minus at least a few hours to sleep), we have become an impatient society. This societal characteristic does not serve the investor well. Successful investing requires patience. It demands the time to develop an investing game plan and the time to research investments adequately. It requires you to wait to purchase an investment until it reaches the price you want to pay. It means fully reviewing the decision to sell an investment before pulling the sell trigger.

5. Be Decisive

Procrastination is the enemy of successful investing. Unfortunately, opportunities for an investor to procrastinate are legion, ranging from not "getting around" to making a financial plan to delaying a stock purchase until tomorrow to "forgetting" to set up an education savings plan for the kids.

If you are a procrastinator, you are less likely to be a successful investor. Universal rule number five for successful investing rejects procrastination. In other words, once you have decided to take action regarding your investments, as Nike proclaims, "Just do it!"

4

Basic Investing Math

Mathematics seems to endow one with something like a new sense.

Charles Darwin

Fortunately, you don't need a university degree in mathematics to be a successful investor. However, understanding the basic math concepts set out below will help you make better investment decisions.

Rule of 72: How Fast Will I Double My Money?

The rule of 72 is a formula for calculating how long it takes to double the value of an investment. It's one of the great tools of investing and it's simple.

Years to double your money = 72 ÷ % rate of return

For example, if you buy a $1,000 bond that earns 4% interest, it will take 18 years (72 ÷ 4 = 18) to double your money if you keep reinvesting the $1,000 plus the interest you get every year.

Every investor should learn the rule of 72 by heart. It's a quick way to get a feel for the value of an investment and its impact on your portfolio.

Compounding Return Rates

The return rate or interest rate is a measure of the profit you make from investing a sum of money. It is usually expressed as an

The essence of compounding - reinvest this year's profit so next year's profit will be paid on both the original investment and the reinvested profit.

annual per cent of the original investment. If the profit or interest you make is reinvested, the next year's profit will be paid on both the original investment and the reinvested profit. This is the essence of compounding money.

If you know the return rate you'll make on an investment, you can figure out the future value of your investment using one of the formulas below.

1. *Simple Interest. No Compounding.* The interest is paid out as it is received:

$$FV = PV \, (1 + ni)$$

2. *Compound Interest.* The interest paid is reinvested at the same interest rate:

$$FV = PV \, (1 + i)^n$$

Where

FV is the future value of the sum of money (the original amount invested plus the reinvested profit)
PV is present value (the original amount of money invested)
i is the interest rate or return rate per year, as a decimal
n is the number of years invested.

Over time, compound investments will make you much more money than simply spending the profit when it arrives every year.

A Few Scenarios

Consider the following real life example of how you can use these formulas to help make investing decisions.

You have $50,000 that you want to save to buy a house in 5 years. You can invest the money in a GIC at a simple annual interest rate of 5% (i = 0.05) or at a compound rate of 4.75% (i = 0.0475). Which is the better choice?

If the interest is paid out every year and not reinvested, in 5 years you will have $62,500 ($50,000 (1 + 5 x 0.05)) and a profit of $12,500.

If you reinvest the profit every year, in 5 years you will have $63,058 ($50,000 (1 + 0.0475))^5 and a profit of $13,058.

So, even though the GIC paying 5% simple interest seems better than the one at 4.75%, you receive over $500 more profit at the end of 5 years if you choose the compound interest investment.

The power of compounding profits over time is spectacularly illustrated by two scenarios that compare the total return from investing $10,000 over two different timeframes. (The compound interest future value formula is used to calculate the total investment return and, for simplicity, taxes and inflation are ignored in these calculations).

a) Jessica inherited $10,000 when her grandmother died. She placed the money in a savings account at 6% interest with automatic reinvestment of the interest. Twenty-five years later, Jessica's savings had grown to $42,919.

b) Suzanne, Jessica's younger sister, promptly spent the inheritance from her grandmother on an exotic vacation and designer clothes. Twenty years later she inherited $10,000 from her great aunt. Older and wiser, she decided to save the money in an account earning 6% interest with automatic reinvestment of the interest. After five years, Suzanne's savings had grown to $13,382.

The graph in Figure 4.1 compares the total investment return (initial investment plus all the interest earned) for each scenario.

Figure 4.1
Total Investment Return for $10,000 Invested at 6% Compound Interest

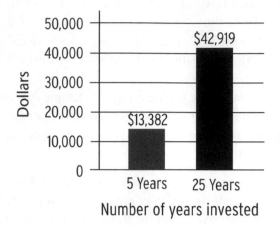

Higher interest rates magnify the extra savings produced by compounding. Invested at 10% interest, the same $10,000 yields $108,347 after 25 years and $16,105 after 5 years!

There is an important lesson here for all investors. Over time, compound interest has a significant positive impact on the value of your investments. Saving sooner definitely pays off!

5

The Educated Investor

Those who cannot learn from history are doomed to repeat it.

George Santayana

Educate Yourself

The successful investor is an educated investor. Even if you rely on the recommendations of a financial advisor, you need sufficient knowledge to be able to evaluate the recommendations to confirm they are in your best interest.

Reading this book and other tomes on investing is a good way to begin your investing education. Courses on investing are offered at community colleges and boards of education night school programs. Brokerage firms hold educational seminars for potential and existing clients. There is much useful information available on the Internet.

However, successful investing is a journey, not a destination. And ongoing investor education is part of this journey. On each leg of your voyage you are searching for new information and advice that will contribute to better investing decisions. But, what information? And whose advice? I'll try to answer these questions in this chapter.

Finding and Evaluating Investing Information

There is definitely no shortage of information on investing available to the public. Sources range from the Internet to newspapers, investment books and newsletters, magazines, business television shows, "free" investment seminars and advice from investment advisors. Unfortunately, much of this information is "investment pornography", information presented in a manner designed to titillate investors and persuade them to invest in things that may or may not be in their best interest.

So, finding investing information is not the problem; finding accurate, objective and useful information is the challenge. To develop the ability to critically analyze investing information and separate the wheat from the chaff, read widely on financial matters including publications with points of view with which you do not agree. And remember to always think for yourself.

A Baker's Dozen Sources of Investing Information

1. *The Internet.* A good place to start your search for investing information is on the Internet. It is amazing what you can find if you know how to search. The key to worthwhile results is to use very specific terms and to narrow the search by placing phrases in quotation marks. My personal favourite search engine is Google. The same search using other search engines will turn up different information. Use different search engines to generate more potentially useful results.

    Basic information on investing is available at investment industry web sites such as the following:

    - Canadian Securities Institute – not-for-profit organization providing education for investors and for the financial services industry (<www.csi.ca>),
    - Investor Education Fund – set up by Ontario Securities Commission (<www.investored.ca>),
    - Advocis' consumer information section (<www.advocis.ca/content/consumers.html>) or

- Canadian Securities Administrators – a forum to coordinate and harmonize regulation of Canadian capital markets (<www.csa-acvm.ca>). It includes links to all 13 provincial/territorial securities regulators. These sites provide investing information oriented toward investors living in a specific province.

2. *Originating Organization.* The most accurate information is provided by the organization which originally created the information. The Internet is an indispensable tool in this regard. Just key the organization's name into an Internet search engine and carefully select its web site from among the many hits. You may need to surf the site to find what you are looking for, but it's probably there. The examples below demonstrate what you can find.
   - What tax relief did the Canadian government provide for investors in its latest budget? To find out, read the government's budget news release and backgrounders in the Media Room section of the Department of Finance web site, <www.fin.gc.ca>.
   - What's the current interest rate on a Canada Savings Bond (CSB)? Just click on "here" in the Rates box on the CSB web site, <www.csb.gc.ca/eng/>.
   - When will Royal Bank issue its next dividend payment? At the bank's web site, <www.rbc.com>, click on Investor Relations, then Stocks and Dividends and then Dividend Dates.
   - What stocks are included in the Saxon Stock Fund? Check out <www.saxonfunds.com>, then click on Funds, then Saxon Stock Funds and then Fund Commentary/Holdings.

3. *Regulatory Agencies.* The information companies are required to file with regulatory agencies is the company's official statement and is generally reliable.

   The company profiles at <www.sedar.com>, the System for Electronic Document Analysis and Retrieval (SEDAR) include all information (from financial statements through press releases and management's discussion of its financial results) that companies have filed to comply with Canadian securities regulations.

In the U.S., American company filings with U.S. securities regulators can be found at the EDGAR (the Electronic Data Gathering, Analysis, and Retrieval system) website, <www.sec.gov/edgar.shtml>.

4. *Rating Services*. Rating services provide useful information on the quality of corporate debt instruments such as bonds and preferred shares. In Canada, you can use the Dominion Bond Rating Service at <www.dbrs.com/intnlweb/>.

5. *Commercial Investor Web Sites*. Well recognized commercial investor web sites are a reasonably reliable source of company and mutual fund information as well as comparative industry data. They are a good way to quickly sift through large volumes of information and identify potential investment opportunities for more detailed consideration. These sites do not always have the most current information and may, on occasion, contain errors.

Commercial investor web sites are often associated with large media organizations. The ones I use most often are the following:
- CNN World Business <edition.cnn.com/BUSINESS/>,
- Canadian Business Online <www.canadianbusiness.com>,
- Canoe Money <www.money.canoe.ca>,
- Globeinvestor <www.globeinvestor.com/>,
- Google Finance <www.google.com/finance>,
- Morningstar Canadian and U.S. sites <www.morningstar.ca> and <www.morningstar.com>,
- MSN Money <moneycentral.msn.com> and
- Yahoo Finance Canada <ca.finance.yahoo.com>.

6. *Reports*. Media and stockbrokerage reports may include detailed analysis of investment opportunities and buy or sell recommendations. These are the subjective opinions of the authors. Never accept these reports at face value. Be very skeptical. Knowing the author's affiliation and motivation for preparing the report is essential to determine its usefulness. For

example, the objective of many brokerage reports is to attract companies to the firm's investment banking business. They may paint an optimistic picture of a company stock that is not a good investment for an individual investor.

7. *Business Shows.* Another source of investing information is business television shows. The Business News Network is available Canada-wide. Major American business networks available in Canada include MSNBC and Bloomberg Television. Some local television stations offer personal investing shows. Don't take the investing recommendations made on such shows as genuine and unbiased. Before investing, do your own research to determine if an investment is right for you.

> Knowing the author's affiliation and motivation for preparing the report is essential to determine its usefulness.

8. *Newspapers.* The business section of your local or regional newspaper may contain useful economic and financial information. These sections often feature regular columns by financial writers such as Ellen Roseman of *The Toronto Star*, Linda Leatherdale of *The Toronto Sun,* Paul Delean of *The Montreal Gazette* and Ray Turchansky of *The Edmonton Journal.* Read the business section regularly over several weeks to gauge its usefulness.

   The nationally published Canadian newspapers, *The Globe and Mail* and *The National Post,* tend to have larger business sections than local papers. They provide detailed national and international investing news and analysis as well as regular personal finance columns by such writers as Rob Carrick *(The Globe and Mail)* and Jonathan Chevreau *(The National Post).*

   The truly dedicated investor may want to read *The Wall Street Journal,* the premier newspaper of the investment business in the U.S.

9. *Investment Newsletters.* I define investment newsletters as regular publications that provide investment advice and do not include advertising. These publications do not generally deliver stock benchmark beating results. A 2006 review of the

performance of hundreds of newsletters in Canada and the U.S. over the last 25 years, reported that only three outperformed the U.S. equity market, as measured by the Wilshire 5000 broad market index.[1] However, these newsletters can be a good source of investing ideas for further investigation.

Canadian-based newsletters that are worth reading include the following:

- *Investment Reporter,* <www.investmentreporter.com>,
- *Money Reporter,* <www.moneyreporter.ca> and
- *The Successful Investor,* <www.thesuccessfulinvestor.com>.

10. *Magazines.* Investing magazines can provide investment ideas, but be skeptical. Most of these publications survive on advertising revenues, a situation that could skew their contents. Furthermore, their columnists may have vested interests in promoting certain investments.

Here are some examples of Canadian investing magazines worth scanning regularly:

- *Canadian Business and Moneysense* – national publications owned by media giant Rogers Communications,
- *Investor's Digest of Canada* – a biweekly tabloid publication owned by investment advice conglomerate MPL Communications and
- *Canadian Moneysaver* – an independently published monthly magazine that does not accept display advertising.

11. *Books.* Books on investing can provide useful information to the individual investor. However, readers beware. Appearance in print is no guarantee that does the information is true.

12. *Clubs.* Investment clubs and discussion groups, such as *Canadian Moneysaver* ShareClubs, can be an important part of an investor's education. Some clubs actually buy and sell investments while others limit themselves to exchanging information and hosting guest speakers.

---

[1] Duncan Hood, "Who can you trust?" *MoneySense*, November 2006.

13. *The Internet, Again.* Internet chat rooms, online forums and blogs are replete with investing information and recommendations. Some postings are worthwhile and are written by knowledgeable authors, some are just plain wrong and others promote schemes to separate naive investors from their money. Be very wary.

Above all, when confronted with any piece of investing information, always remember to apply universal investing rule number one: Think for yourself.

Part II

Financial Service Providers

6

Hire a Financial Advisor or Be Your Own Advisor?

A fool thinks he needs no advice, but a wise man listens to others.

Proverbs 12:15

If you are like the average Canadian, you want and need help with your investments. Your challenge is to find the right hired help. This chapter will explain how to choose the right help, a financial advisor who suits your personal circumstances.

In the marketplace, most financial services companies offer individual investors a bundled package of investment advice and investment transaction services. Whether or not you opt for one of these bundles, you need to think of these two services separately in order to make the best investment decisions for your personal situation.

To reinforce the need to evaluate financial advisors separately from financial transaction services, I have written distinct chapters on these topics. For a complete picture of these two related areas of investing, read both chapters.

What is a Financial Advisor?

For purposes of this book, I define a financial advisor as someone who is paid to provide investment advice and, in some cases, to manage investments for the person who pays for the advice, the client.

Entire books have been written on how to choose a financial advisor. In my opinion, this is overkill given that there are only a few choices for obtaining financial advice.

1. Be your own financial advisor, i.e., hire yourself.

2. Hire a financial advisor who does not sell financial products and is paid by charging the client a fee for service.

3. Hire a financial advisor who is associated with a stockbroker, bank, deposit broker, insurance company or mutual fund company that sells financial products. These advisors are paid in one or more of the following ways:
   • annual fee paid directly by the client based on a percentage of assets under management,
   • commissions paid by the client when investments are bought or sold,
   • commissions paid by a financial products company for sales of the company's products,
   • annual trailer fees from mutual fund companies based on a percentage of the value of the company's funds held in accounts of the advisor's clients,
   • salary paid by the advisor's employer or
   • bonus paid by the advisor's employer for meeting sales targets.

4. Use a financial advisor for part of your portfolio and be your own advisor for the remainder. To do so, you'll need more than one investment account and thus will have access to investing information from different financial service providers. Over time, as your investing knowledge and self-confidence improve, you can invest a larger proportion of your investments acting as your own advisor.

Choosing a financial advisor is a bit like committing to a marriage.

Twelve Steps to Choosing the Right Financial Advisor

Choosing a financial advisor is a bit like committing to a marriage. You want to get it right because divorce is painful. To help you avoid the pain, use the following guide to select the financial advisor who is right for you.

1. Decide how much time and effort you are honestly committed to spending to:
   • become knowledgeable about investing,
   • keep current on financial matters and the stock market and
   • set up and maintain your investing portfolio.

   Be brutally honest with yourself. Will you really dedicate the time to become sufficiently knowledgeable about financial matters to be your own financial advisor? Do you have the time to keep current on investing issues? Do you have the personal discipline to monitor your investments on an ongoing basis, reach decisions to buy or sell investments and then act on these decisions?

   Remember to apply universal investing rule number two: Know yourself when deciding whether or not to act as your own financial advisor.

   If you are a disciplined person who will spend the necessary time, then being your own financial advisor is an option.

2. Decide how much money you have to invest now and estimate how much additional money you will be investing over the next few years. You'll need to know these numbers because some financial advisors only accept clients with a certain minimum amount of money to invest.

3. If you don't have a complete financial plan that covers all aspects of your personal finances, consider completing one before proceeding with the selection of a financial advisor for your investments. For this task, I recommend using a professional financial planner such as a person who holds the Certified Financial Planner (CFP) designation. You can search for a CFP in good standing at The Financial Planners Standards Council's web site <www.cfp-ca.org>.

4. Write down what you expect a financial advisor to do for you. Typical expectations for a financial advisor might include some or all of the items listed here.

   - Provide a written overall investment strategy that includes realistic projected return rates and meets the client's particular needs and objectives.
   - Provide specific investment recommendations (purchase and sale) consistent with the client's investment strategy and the reasons for the recommendation, including the risks and benefits.
   - Answer any questions about investing and provide ongoing education about investing.
   - Provide advice on the tax implications of different types of investments including those he/she recommends.
   - Provide referrals to other professionals, such as an insurance agent or tax accountant, where appropriate to meet the client's investing needs.
   - Be easily accessible by telephone.
   - Call monthly with an update.
   - Meet quarterly to review the client's investments.
   - Contact clients promptly if current events (e.g., stock market crash, a sudden sizeable rise in interest rates) have a major impact on their investments.
   - Conduct the purchase and sale of investments in a timely manner at the best available price.
   - Provide clear, understandable and complete written statements of the client's investments and return rates.
   - Disclose all costs, commissions and fees the client pays.

Read your list of expectations and decide if you are still committed to acting as your own financial advisor. If you are, you can stop here and move to the next chapter.

5. Make a list of questions for a potential financial advisor. Here are some examples of the questions you should ask.
   - What are your qualifications? Look for:
     - a financial designation or designations that fit your specific needs (the major designations are listed in Figure 6.1);
     - several years of experience as a financial advisor;
     - knowledgeable in tax laws, as tax plays a major role in the success of your investments;
     - licensed to sell at least mutual funds and fixed income products like GICs, as well as any other types of investments (stocks, bonds, etc.) of interest to you;
     - committed to ongoing education and upgrading and
     - strong communication skills.
   - How long have you been a financial advisor?
   - Who else is on your team? Who is your backup if you're not in the office or on vacation?
   - How long has your firm been in business? Is the firm a member of an investor protection insurance fund?
   - Does your firm sell investments as well as provide advice? If so, what products (stocks, bonds, brands of mutual funds) are offered?
   - What is your investment philosophy?
   - Do you personally buy and sell financial products for clients? If so, what products (stocks, bonds, mutual funds, options, etc.) are you qualified to sell and what products do you typically recommend?
   - Do you prepare an investment plan for each of your clients based on each client's personal situation?
   - How often will we talk and/or meet? Where will our meetings be held?
   - How quickly will you respond if I call or email you?
   - How are you paid? What fees does your firm charge for account administration?

- What research, newsletters, etc., do you and your firm provide to clients? Do you hold educational seminars for clients?
- What kind of account statements do you provide and how frequently?
- How will I know how well my investments are performing? What performance benchmarks do you use?
- Do you provide statements with the original cost, current market value and return rate of each investment? Will you provide me with an annual return rate for my overall portfolio?
- What is your firm's procedure for handling client complaints?

Note you may want to hire more than one advisor, particularly if you have special needs. If so, I think it's best to have a principal advisor and hire specialist advisors, as needed.

6. Develop a list of potential advisors. Here are some ways to identify candidates.
   - Canvas your family, friends and business associates to get the names of advisors they would recommend.
   - Find out what financial advisors are available at the bank where you have your account.
   - Consult the "find an advisor" section of the web site of professional financial advisor organizations.
   - Scan the financial media (business section of newspapers, financial web sites, magazines, etc.) for articles referencing or written by financial advisors.
   - Attend a financial forum or seminars presented by investment advisors of brokerage firms.

7. Sift through the leads you have amassed and make a short list of two or three advisors. Use the questions you have drafted to assist in selecting the candidates.

8. Interview all the advisors on your short list. Ask each candidate the same questions and take notes on how each one answers.

9. Take some time to reflect on the interviews and review your interview notes before selecting the best candidate.

10. Perform your due diligence. Confirm that the chosen advisor and his/her firm have the qualifications and provide the services they have indicated that they offer. The organizations that offer the professional financial designations listed in the table in Figure 6.1 are useful in this regard. These organizations usually have a web site that includes a list of members in good standing, qualifications for membership, their code of business conduct and what to do if you have a complaint.

11. Contact the chosen advisor, indicate your interest in hiring him/her and arrange a meeting to further discuss and finalize your relationship.

   Request that the advisor provide a written agreement, usually called an investment policy statement, detailing the terms you have agreed upon. The agreement should cover such things as:
   • the level of risk you are willing to take,
   • the target asset allocation, allowable range in each asset class and process for maintaining the targeted allocation,
   • the range of the expected return rate of your portfolio,
   • any investment restrictions,
   • all fees and when they are charged,
   • frequency and nature of contact with the advisor (e.g., telephone, email, meetings) and
   • reporting on the performance of your investments including benchmarks used for comparison.

Note that some advisors offer a number of fee options. Many are willing to negotiate their compensation to get your business. You need to determine what is best for you, given the amount of money you have to invest and your investment philosophy. Don't just accept the first fees quoted.

12. After 6 months with the new advisor, review the advisor's performance and decide if he/she has met your expectations. If not, consider hiring the advisor who came second in your original search or return to step 6 and prepare a new list of potential advisors. If you are not satisfied, do not hesitate to change advisors. The new advisor should take care of the paper work required to transfer your account.

Figure 6.1

Financial Designations which Canadian Investment Advisors May Hold

Canadian Investment Manager, CIM
Certified Financial Planner, CFP
Certified General Accountant, CGA
Certified Management Accountant, CMA
Certified Senior Advisor, CSA
Chartered Accountant, CA
Chartered Life Underwriter, CLU
Chartered Financial Analyst, CFA
Chartered Financial Consultant, ChFC
Elder Planning Counsellor, EPC
Fellow of the Canadian Securities Institute, FCSI
Personal Financial Planner, PFP
Professional Retirement Planner, PRP
Registered Financial Planner, RFP
Registered Health Underwriter, RHU
Trust and Estate Practitioner, TEP

Closing Thoughts on Financial Advisors

You must understand how your financial advisor is paid as this will significantly impact the financial advice received. The situations below illustrate why this is important.

- Advisors who are paid by commission will usually recommend mutual funds that pay the highest fees to advisors. Higher fees mean increased fund expenses and hence lower returns for investors.
- Advisors may advise clients to buy and sell stocks more frequently than necessary in order to generate commissions.
- Advisors who work at companies that sell new stock issues (called IPOs or initial public offerings) may recommend an IPO to clients because the firm wants to unload the stock in its inventory, not because it is the best investment for the client.

You must carefully evaluate what a potential financial advisor offers before hiring the advisor. And your job doesn't end once you have a financial advisor. Always critically assess the advice your advisor provides and decide for yourself if this advice will advance your investment goals.

7

Service Providers for Investment Transactions

To give real service you must add something which cannot be bought or measured with money, and that is sincerity and integrity.

Douglas Adams

The marketplace is awash with financial firms of all stripes ready to provide you with investment transaction services for a fee. Many, but not all, of these companies offer financial advice along with the transaction services. If you invest, you will need to deal with one of these companies. The trick is to pick the company that offers the best combination of price and the services you truly need.

In this chapter, you'll read about the categories of investment transaction service providers doing business in Canada. Use my Checklist for Evaluating Firms Providing Investment Transaction Services, at the end of this chapter, to develop your specific needs for investment transactions. Evaluate potential service providers against your list to find the company that is right for you.

Full Service Investment Firms

The major Canadian banks all have divisions which offer individualized financial advice and the widest selection of investment products including stocks, bonds, mutual funds, cash products such as GICs, new stock issues, options and more exotic investments such as options and flow through shares. Other full service firms include Canaccord Capital, Credential Securities, Desjardins Securities, Edward Jones and Investors Group.

If you deal with a full service firm, you have a dedicated financial advisor who provides research, advice, ongoing customer service and can offer you the widest selection of investment products. Full service firm financial advisors also take care of all investment transactions for clients.

Financial advisors at full service firms do not always provide impartial advice. They may be required to support other divisions of the firm by selling new stock issues to their clients, even if they do not believe in the stock. Advisors paid by commission or by trailer fees are inclined to provide advice that puts the most dollars in their pockets.

Using a full service firm to buy and sell investments is the most expensive option. Trading fees for stocks are relatively high, around 2% of the value of the stock. Mutual funds may be sold with a sales commission. GIC rates are usually not the highest available in the marketplace. Some advisors charge clients an all-inclusive annual fee (usually a percentage of the value of assets in an account), which includes trading costs.

Full service firms usually are interested only in accepting new clients who have at least $50,000 to $100,000 to invest.

Full service investment firms and discount brokers are members of the Investment Dealers Association of Canada <www.ida.ca>, the national self-regulatory trade association for the Canadian securities industry.

Discount Brokers

Discount brokers offer similar products as full service investment firms but they usually do not offer investment advice. They are essentially order takers. You can invest by telephone or set up an Internet account to carry out online investment transactions, such as buying and selling stocks and mutual funds. Their web sites offer tutorials on online transactions. Research may be available and there may be a charge for this service.

Discount broker trading fees for stocks vary. The brokers owned by the major banks charge $25 to $30 to buy or sell up to

Not all discount brokers are members of the Canadian Deposit Insurance Fund.

one thousand shares. Discounts for larger accounts and high volume traders may be available. Smaller firms, such as E*Trade, eNorthern, Questrade and Interactive Brokers, have lower fees and focus on offering the fastest trades. Mutual funds can generally be purchased without fees if they are held for a minimum time period (usually 90 days). Like the full service firms, GIC rates are usually not the highest available in the marketplace.

Note that not all discount brokers are members of the Canadian Deposit Insurance Fund, which offers insurance against financial losses by customers of a member company that declares bankruptcy. (See Chapter 23 on insurance for more details.)

The minimum investment at a discount broker is in the $5,000 to $15,000 range.

As noted above, discount brokers are members of the Investment Dealers Association of Canada <www.ida.ca>.

Branches of Banks, Trust Companies and Credit Unions

Most bank, trust company and credit union branches sell GICs, savings bonds and mutual funds. Financial advisors may be available to assist you. The advice offered is frequently based on standard portfolios of in-house financial products. Fees for mutual funds depend on the fund purchased with the in-house brand usually sold without commission.

Account minimums can be as low as the $100 it takes to buy a Canada Savings Bond.

The web sites of the relevant trade associations have lots of information about these institutions:

- Canadian Bankers Association <www.cba.ca> and
- Credit Union Central of Canada <www.cucentral.ca>.

Deposit Brokers/Agents

Deposit brokers are independent retail businesses that specialize in cash or cash equivalent investments such as term deposits and

Canadian Savings Bonds. They may also sell mutual funds and insurance products. Deposit brokers are compensated by the financial institutions that supply the products they sell, so clients do not pay a direct transaction fee. Minimum account size can be as low as $500.

You can find out more about deposit brokers by contacting the Federation of Canadian Independent Deposit Brokers at <www.fcidb.com>.

Mutual Fund Companies

You can buy mutual funds through the service providers discussed above. As well, most non-bank owned mutual fund companies offer individual investors direct purchase of their funds without sales commissions. Financial advisors may be available to assist in setting up an investment portfolio of the company's mutual funds.

Minimum initial purchases vary significantly, depending on the company and range from about $5,000 (e.g., Saxon Funds) to $150,000 (e.g., ABC Funds) or more.

The Investment Funds Institute of Canada is the trade association of the mutual fund industry in Canada <www.ific.ca>.

The Mutual Fund Dealers Association of Canada is the national self-regulatory organization for distributors of mutual funds in Canada <www.mfda.ca>.

Private Investment Counsel/Portfolio Management

There are firms in Canada dedicated solely to the management of the investments of their clients. They provide financial advice and take care of all investment transactions. These firms focus on high net worth individuals. The minimum account size is $100,000 to $150,000, with many firms requiring $500,000. Fees are generally 1-2% of assets under management plus custodial fees.

You can find out more about these firms by contacting The Investment Counsel Association of Canada, the trade association of these firms <www.investmentcounsel.org>.

Share Purchase Plans (SPP) and Dividend Reinvestment Plans (DRIP)

A limited number of Canadian companies and about 1,000 U.S. companies offer a Dividend Reinvestment Plan or DRIP that automatically reinvests shareholder's dividends in additional shares. The shares must be registered in the shareowner's name, not the broker's name (for trading convenience the shares in most investment accounts are held in the brokerage firm's name).

Some companies also have Share Purchase Plans (SPP). SPPs allow shareholders to purchase stock directly from the company at no cost or for a low acquisition fee.

While you save transaction fees and are able to take advantage of the compounding effect of dividend reinvesting, SPPs and DRIPs aren't for everyone. Setting up these plans takes some work and includes the cost and effort of obtaining a share registered in your name. As well, SPP and DRIP investors need to be disciplined administrators to ensure that they have the records of their DRIP and SPP investments needed for income tax purposes.

There is extensive coverage of DRIPs and SPPs at the DRIP Investing Resource Centre web site, <www.dripinvesting.org>.

Canadians interested in buying U.S. DRIPs and SPPs should consider reading:

- the monthly newsletter, *The DRIP Investor* <dripinvestor.com/index.asp> and
- *Buying U.S. Stocks Without A Broker: A Canadian* investor's *guide to buying U.S. stocks direct – without a broker – via "No Load Stocks"* by Charles Coulson. Horizon Publishing Company, 2007.

Synthetic Dividend Reinvestment Plans

Some investment firms allow clients to reinvest dividends, received from certain companies or mutual funds, into additional shares or units. This useful service is offered free or at low cost, reduces your commission costs and ensures that dividend dollars are promptly reinvested.

If you want to participate in one of these plans, you need to request that this option be activated for your investment account.

Wrap Accounts

A wrap account is sold as a one-stop investment solution for those who are too busy or unable to take care of their investments. It combines or "wraps" investment services into one fee, usually about 1-3% of the value of assets under management. Wrap services and fees vary depending on the service provider but usually include financial advice, portfolio design, maintaining the right mix of investments, buy and sell transactions and account administration and reporting. Most financial services companies offer these accounts dressed up with fancy names, such as RBC Select (RBC), Matchmaker (Bank of Montreal) and Scotia Partners (Bank of Nova Scotia).

Traditional wrap accounts are the most expensive and offer a full range of investments (stocks, bonds, GICs, mutual funds, etc.) and financial advice tailored to the client's specific needs. These fees may be tax deductible as an investment expense.

Mutual fund wrap accounts offer only mutual funds and limited financial advice. A client's money is allocated to one of several standard portfolios based on the client's risk profile. These standard portfolios are selected from mutual funds that vary by asset class and investment style to produce different risk levels.

Financial advisors love wrap accounts: instead of the up and down world of commissions, they get a steady stream of income whether or not the client buys or sells investments and whether or not he/she makes a reasonable return. The wrap fee calculation usually includes the value of any mutual funds in the account. That's like adding another 1-3% to the expense fees that mutual funds already charge! Plus, the advisor could receive ongoing trailer fees from the fund company as long as the client holds the fund.[1]

I am not a fan of wrap accounts. I think the fees are too high for the service provided. If you buy quality investments, you will not sell them frequently. So, the better choice is to pay the commission

---

[1] WRAP accounts should hold mutual funds designed for such accounts. These funds have lower fees than regular funds to compensate for the fact that the advisor is already paid by wrap fees.

for the purchase transaction and pay separately for financial advice.

If you decide that you need the one stop convenience of a wrap account, make sure that you fully understand exactly what you are getting before signing up. And don't forget to negotiate the fees. Traditional wrap account providers will likely reduce their fees to get your business, especially if you have a sizable amount of money to invest.

Closing Thoughts on Investment Transaction Service Providers

Whichever company you choose to handle your investment transactions, investigate and confirm its qualifications before becoming a customer. You can do this easily by seeing if the company is a member in good standing of the relevant trade association (see the association web sites listed in the previous sections). These associations typically have membership requirements including codes of business conduct, procedures for filing complaints regarding a member and a list of current members. There may also be requirements for members to carry investor protection insurance.

Most reputable companies are members of their industry trade association. If a firm is not a member, be particularly vigilant.

> Whichever company you choose, investigate and confirm its qualifications before becoming a customer.

Checklist for Evaluating Investment Transaction Service Providers

1. Adequate range of investments (stocks, bonds, mutual funds, GICs, etc.)

2. Customer service – reputation and record of complaints

3. Hours of operation

4. Account administrative fees – smaller accounts may be charged annual RRSP fees and account maintenance fees

5. Commissions to buy and sell stocks, funds and bonds

6. Cash transfers to other accounts or institutions available and the cost of transfers

7. Online account access and capabilities:
   - online access provides up-to-date account information
   - support is available if technical problems occur
   - ease of use for research and buying and selling online

8. Account statements:
   - Easy-to-understand content includes holdings, current value, book value (for capital gains calculations), rate of return and performance of relevant benchmarks
   - Frequency and delivery method (mail, email, online)

9. Research on stocks, mutual funds and economic reports – availability and cost, if any

10. Education and financial planning tools

11. Account security and track record of security breaches

12. Privacy policy and track record for protecting customers' personal information

13. Trade association membership

14. Investor protection insurance

8

Resolving Problems with Financial Services Providers

The stock market is filled with individuals who know the price of everything, but the value of nothing.

Philip Fisher, *Common Stocks Uncommon Profits*

Life isn't perfect. All of us occasionally run into problems with businesses that provide services. Perhaps your local auto repair shop charged hundreds of dollars, but didn't fix your car properly. Or, maybe the contractor who renovated your kitchen did a shoddy job. Individuals and businesses providing financial services are no different. Sometimes, there are problems. For example, you receive an incorrect investment account statement or you discover that your investment advisor has bought stocks for your account without your permission.

Problems with Financial Advisors

If you have a problem with a financial advisor, you should first try to resolve the complaint directly with the person. If this is unsuccessful, contact the customer care or customer relations department of the firm that employs the advisor. If this fails, there are two approaches to further escalate your complaint:

- follow the complaint processes for financial services firms (see the following paragraphs), or

- get in touch with the advisor's professional association. These associations have codes of conduct for members and a procedure for handling complaints filed against its members.

Problems with Financial Services Firms

If you have a problem with a financial services firm, contact the customer care or customer relations department of the firm. The next level of escalation is the firm's ombudsman if the organization is a bank or its compliance department if it is an investment firm.

Taking the Problem to the Top

But what to do if that doesn't work? Fortunately, there is external help available if you cannot resolve a problem with a financial services provider. The provincial securities commission that administers securities laws in the province where you live is a good starting point for guidance on filing investing related complaints within that province. See the Canadian Securities Administrator's web site, <www.csa-acvm.ca>, for a list of all 13 provincial and territorial securities commissions.

> Fortunately, there is external help available if you cannot resolve a problem with a financial services provider.

If your financial services provider is a member of a self-regulated organization, such as the Investment Dealers Association of Canada or the Mutual Fund Dealers Association of Canada, you can contact the relevant association. Each such association has a procedure for handling complaints regarding its members.

The Ombudsman for Banking Services and Investments (OBSI) is an independent organization that investigates customer complaints against banks and other deposit-taking organizations, investment dealers, mutual fund dealers and mutual fund companies.

Web site	www.obsi.ca
Telephone	1-888-451-4519
	In Toronto (416) 287-2877
Email	ombudsman@obsi.ca

Mail   Ombudsman for Banking Services and Investments
        P.O. Box 896
        Station Adelaide
        Toronto, ON
        M5C 2K3

The Canadian Life and Health Insurance OmbudService (CLHIO) is an independent service that assists consumers with concerns and complaints about life and health insurance products and services. This includes investment products such as segregated funds and annuities provided by insurance companies.

Web site   www.clhio.ca
Telephone   1-800-268-8099,
                Toronto (416) 777-2344
Email   Access via the web site
Mail   CAC
        20 Toronto Street, Suite 710
        Toronto, ON
        M5C 2B8

In addition, you may want to contact the Small Investor Protection Association (SIPA), a volunteer member organization committed to fair practice in the investment industry. The SIPA web site includes useful guidance on the process for handling complaints about investments with a bank, broker, financial advisor or other seller of financial products.

Web site   www.sipa.ca
Telephone   905-471-2911
Email   SIPA@sipa.ca
Mail   Small Investor Protection Association
        P.O. Box 325
        Markham, ON
        L3P 3J8

If you have a problem with a financial services provider, remember to:

- Pursue your complaint promptly and courteously.
- Check the web site of the regulatory organization governing the provider at issue for details on how to handle complaints that fall within its bailiwick.
- Keep written records of all communications regarding the problem including all correspondence and details and dates of any conversations.
- Don't give up.

Part III

Investment Possibilities and Profits

9

Types of Investments and Profit Expectations

When it is a question of money, everybody is of the same religion.

Voltaire

Asset Classes

The investment industry groups various types of investments into what are known as asset classes. The three traditional asset classes are stocks, bonds and cash/cash equivalents. Today many others are available. These so called alternative investments include real estate, hedge funds, options, foreign exchange, gold bullion and even fine art. These assets are defined and discussed in detail in later chapters of this book.

Each asset class has specific risk characteristics. In general, the potential return rate of an asset class is directly proportional to its risk level. The relative risks of various asset classes and sub-classes are listed in Figure 9.1.

Figure 9.1
Asset Classes and Relative Risk

Asset Class	Risk Level
Cash, T-bills, GICs, government savings bonds, money market funds	
Government bonds	
Mortgages	Increasing
Corporate bonds	risk of no
Debentures	profit and
Preferred shares	losing your
Dividend paying common shares	investment
Common shares without dividends	
Shares of start up companies	
Alternative investments – real estate, options, hedge funds, precious metals, fine art, etc.	

Benchmarks for Measuring Investing Performance

Good benchmarks closely resemble the investment being evaluated and are clearly defined.

When the rate of return of an investment is analyzed, the performance is usually compared to a benchmark. In the investing world, a benchmark (usually called a benchmark index) is a feasible alternative to the investment(s) being evaluated. Good benchmarks closely resemble the investment being evaluated and are clearly defined.

Figure 9.2 lists some of the best-known investing benchmarks. There are many others and new benchmarks are proposed regularly. For an extensive list of benchmarks, see globefund.com's web page, <www.globefund.com/v5/content/help/faq-charts-indexes.html>.

Traditionally, stock market index construction has been based on market capitalization – the per cent of each stock in the index is based on its market capitalization or market value (number of shares issued multiplied by the stock price). So, a large company with a big stock market value can greatly impact an index. For example, at the height of the technology stock mania in 2000, Nortel Networks represented 30% of the Toronto Stock Exchange (TSE) 300 Index. When this stock crashed 25.5% on October 25, 2000, the Index plunged 840.3 points or 8.12%, the largest point drop in TSE history.

Consider the S&P/TSX 60 Index, a widely quoted benchmark of Canadian stocks. What does it really represent? This Index consists of the 60 largest and most heavily traded companies on the TSX, the largest Canadian stock exchange. It is a market capitalization index. So, natural resources and financial companies, the biggest companies in Canada, account for almost 50% of the Index. Consequently, this Index does not reflect the performance of many small Canadian companies or all sectors of the Canadian economy.

More recently, with the increased popularity of exchange-traded funds based on benchmark indices, additional approaches for establishing indices have appeared. These newer indices are constructed based on some fundamental characteristics of stocks as opposed to market capitalization. For example, the FTSE RAFI US 1000 Index is composed of the top 1,000 U.S. listed companies by fundamental value. This value is determined by evaluating four factors: total cash dividends, free cash flow, total sales and book equity value.

Fundamental indices avoid some of the problems of capitalization indices. Overvalued stocks are not overweighted and undervalued stocks are not underweighted. As well, Exchange-Traded Funds (ETF) based on these indices are less influenced by market fluctuations not related to actual attributes of the stock.

If you intend to use a benchmark index to analyze the performance of your portfolio or to select an index mutual fund or an ETF, check what stocks are in the index and how it is constructed to confirm that the index fits your portfolio.

Given the volatility of some investments over the short term, benchmarks are most useful for evaluating longer term (at least a year) investment returns.

Figure 9.2

Some Common Investing Benchmarks

Benchmark	Composition/Description
Canada	
S&P/TSX 60 Index	60 largest stocks on the TSX
Universe Bond Index, formerly Scotia Capital Universe Bond Index	921 bonds representing the broad Canadian bond market
S&P/TSX Global Gold Index	Securities of global gold sector, stocks selected by S&P
U.S.	
Dow Jones Industrial Average	Price weighted index of 30 large industrial companies
S&P 500 Index	500 large cap stocks chosen to represent 75% of market
Russell 2000 Index	2,000 U.S. based small cap stocks, represents less than 10% of U.S. market
Russell 3000 Index	3,000 U.S. based stocks, represents about 98% of U.S. market, proxy for broad market
Lehman Brothers U.S. Aggregate Index	Total U.S. investment grade bond market
International	
MSCI Europe, Australasia and Far East Index	Over 1,000 stocks, about 85% of market capitalization of 21 developed countries in Europe, Australia and Asia
MSCI country indices for 56 countries	Stocks representing 85% of the market cap in the specified country

Expected Return Rates and Volatility

Predicting future performance based on the past performance of an investment is never a sure thing. However, historical return rates can provide investors with an indication of the approximate return rate for an asset class. Long-term historical return rates are available for the three traditional asset classes: stocks, bonds and cash and are summarized in Figure 9.3. Such data are not readily obtainable for alternative investments, in part because many of the investments in this class are recent creations.

Figure 9.3

Historical Rates of Return for Traditional Asset Classes

Asset Class	Avg. Annual Return Rate, 1926-2002*	Benchmark Proxy Used	Relative Risk of Loss	Relative Volatility of Returns
Stocks	10.2%	S&P 500 Index	Higher	Higher
Bonds	5.4%	U.S. bonds (2-10 year)	Medium	Medium
Cash	3.8%	U.S. Treasury Bills	Lower	Lower

* Ibbotson Associates, 2003 yearbook as quoted on AOL Money web site.

These data are based on U.S. benchmarks; Canadian asset classes will have similar return rates. Note that the higher the expected return rate, the riskier the investment and the greater the volatility of returns.

You can use expected return rates to estimate the overall return rate of your investments and develop timelines for achieving your investment goals.

10

Asset Allocation

Why not invest your assets in the companies you really like? As Mae West said, "Too much of a good thing can be wonderful."

Warren Buffett

Why Asset Allocation?

Asset allocation means dividing your investments among the various classes of assets introduced in Chapter 9. Allocating assets correctly among various asset classes is responsible for much of a portfolio's return over the long term according to two studies.

- A study published in the Financial Analysts Journal[1] found that about 90% of the variability of returns of a typical mutual fund across time is explained by the fund's asset allocation policy.
- The investment results of 91 very large pension funds, ranging in size from $100 million to well over $3 billion, were examined over a 10-year period ending in 1983.[2] Using market-index returns for stocks, bonds and cash asset classes, the authors looked at four elements that could contribute to investment returns:

---

[1] Roger G. Ibbotson and Paul D. Kaplan, "Does Asset Allocation Policy Explain 40 Percent, 90 Percent, or 100 Percent of Performance?" *Financial Analysts Journal*, January/February 2000.

[2] Gary P. Brinson, L. Randolph Hood, and Gilbert Beebower, "Determinants of Portfolio Performance" *Financial Analysts Journal*, July-August 1986.

- asset allocation,
- individual security selection,
- market timing and
- investing costs.

How you allocate investment dollars will significantly affect the return rate of your investments.

The authors were able to explain 93.6% of a pension fund's performance based solely on knowing its asset allocation policy.

While these studies are based on large institutional funds, I believe that there is a lesson here for the individual investor: how you allocate investment dollars will significantly affect the return rate of your investments.

What is the Right Asset Allocation for You?

The above studies suggest that to be a successful investor you must pay particular attention to correctly allocating your investments among the various classes of assets. The obvious question is – What is the right allocation?

The answer is that it depends on your personal situation. You need to consider a number of points.

- *Your Financial Situation.* How much money do you have to invest? How much money is in your other savings? How secure is your job?
- *Your Investing Time Horizon.* Stock returns fluctuate in the short term. The shorter the investing time frame, the less money you should invest in stocks.
- *Your Tolerance for Risk.* How much money are you prepared to lose if the stock market falls?
- *Your Financial Knowledge and Interest.*
- *Your Investing Objectives.*

By diversifying your investments within a specific asset class, you can further improve returns and reduce risk. This could mean, for example, owning stocks from different countries and several industry sectors. Diversification will be discussed in more detail in the chapters on specific asset classes (Part IV).

To provide you with an idea of how investment assets might be allocated in a typical portfolio, Figure 10.1 sets out sample asset allocation portfolios and approximate return rates for various levels of risk. These examples range from a conservative portfolio focused on protection of capital to an aggressive growth portfolio more suitable for higher risk, longer term investing.

Some investment institutions have developed asset allocation calculators for clients. These calculators ask a series of questions regarding your personal situation and calculate a suggested asset allocation based on your responses. Your financial advisor should be well versed in the subject of asset allocation and be able to provide recommendations on the appropriate asset allocation for your personal situation.

Asset allocation of your investments after retirement is discussed in Chapter 21 Retirement and Investing.

Most asset allocation models focus on stocks, bonds and cash. You may want to include alternative investments, such as real estate, in your investment mix. To manage the high risk of these investments, alternative assets should form only a small portion of your portfolio.

Asset allocation models and calculators are guidelines to consider when developing your investment plan. As you flesh out the asset allocation that works for you, pay particular attention to two of the universal investing rules.

- Think for yourself.
- Know yourself.

Once you have decided on the mix of assets that will meet your investment goals, the next step is to choose specific investments within each asset class. In the coming chapters, I'll delve into each asset class and how to select particular investments. But first, a word about taxes, inflation and your investments.

Figure 10.1
Sample Asset Allocation Portfolios

	Portfolio Description	Cash & Cash Equiv.	Bonds-Canadian or GICs	Bonds-Foreign	Equities-Developed Markets*	Real Estate	Equities Emerging Markets	Estimated Return** %	
	Asset Type (Numbers indicate per cent of total portfolio)								
Income	Lower risk, Capital protection, Current income	5	55	10	30	0	0	6.8	
Income Focused	Moderate risk, Capital protection, Short time horizon	5	50	5	35	5	0	7.2	Increasing Risk, Volatility & Investing Time Horizon →
Balanced	Moderate risk, Capital protection, Medium time horizon	5	40	5	45	5	0	7.7	
Growth	Higher risk, Capital appreciation, Long time horizon	5	20	5	60	5	5	8.7	
Aggressive Growth	Highest risk, Capital appreciation, Long time horizon	5	5	5	70	10	5	9.4	

*Stocks of Canada, United States, Western Europe, Australia, New Zealand, Japan; stocks of other countries are emerging market equities.

**Based on data in Figure 9.3 and assuming real estate returns are equal to stock returns.

11

Taxes, Inflation and Investing: Did You Really Make a Profit?

*For all long term investors, there is only one objective –
maximum total real returns after taxes.*

Sir John Templeton

In the previous chapters, I talked about the potential returns to be made from various types of investments. That's only half the investing story. The other half is the amount of money a Canadian resident gets to keep after the taxman has been paid and inflation or deflation has been accounted for.

Types of Income and Tax Rates

Different types of investment income attract different tax rates. Some types are definitely superior to others as illustrated in Figure 11.1. Capital gains are the profit made when assets such as shares, bonds or land are sold. They provide the best after-tax return. Dividends are a portion of a company's profits that are paid to shareholders as owners of a company. Eligible dividends[1] from Canadian corporations yield almost as much after tax-return as capital gains. Depending on your marginal tax rate, the after-tax returns from these two types of income could be over 2% more than the equivalent interest income.

---

[1]Some Canadian corporations issue non-eligible dividends, which are taxed differently. They tend to be small businesses without publicly traded shares.

Given the way that the Canada Revenue Agency (CRA) taxes the various types of income, you should consider:

- the tax treatment of the potential income from an investment as an integral part of the decision to invest,
- putting investments producing fully taxed income in tax sheltered investments (RRSP/RRIF) and
- putting investments producing Canadian dividends and capital gains in non-registered investing accounts.

Figure 11.1

After-Tax Return Rate for Various Types of Income*

Type of Income	Tax Treatment	Tax Rate, %**	Income Net of Tax, $	After Tax Rate of Return, %
Interest	Fully taxed at your marginal tax rate	46.41	53.59	5.36
Eligible dividends from taxable Canadian corporations	Gross up and dividend tax credit applied to compensate for tax already paid by corporation	24.64	75.36	7.54
Dividends, from foreign corporations	Fully taxed at your marginal tax rate	46.41	53.59	5.36
Capital gains	50% of net capital gains taxable at your marginal tax rate	23.20	76.80	7.68

* The example includes federal and provincial tax and assumes that an Ontario resident invests $1000 which produces $100 of investment income and that the investor's marginal tax rate is 46.41% (the highest marginal tax rate).

** Income tax rates for 2007 as reported by <www.taxtips.ca>.

Tax Deductions and Tax Credits

The Canadian government offers a range of income tax deductions and income tax credits designed to address various public policy issues. You should structure your investments to take full advantage of these tax deductions and credits and improve your investment returns. The major ones to consider are:

- RRSP contribution deduction,
- Canadian dividend tax credit and
- pension income tax credit.

Income Splitting

There are legal ways to move income from a higher earner in a family to a lower earner and reduce the overall income tax bill paid by the family. This works because Canada has a graduated system of income tax – the more you earn, the greater the percentage of your income that goes to taxes. Below are some examples of income splitting.

- Contribute to a Registered Education Savings Plan (RESP) for your child. The income earned in the RESP is only taxed once it is paid out for qualifying education purposes. Your child will be taxed on the RESP income while he/she is a student and likely has little income.
- The higher earning spouse makes an RRSP contribution to his/her spouse's RRSP and then claims the RRSP deduction on their income tax return.
- Parents give gifts to their adult children. The children pay the tax on any income generated by the gift.
- The higher income spouse pays the family expenses and the other spouse invests his/her earnings. Any investment income is taxed at the lower earner's tax rate.
- Allocate half your eligible pension income to your spouse.

You should consider the applicability of income-splitting strategies to your personal situation. The rules around income splitting can be tricky so be fully informed before acting. Consulting a tax specialist will reduce the chance that CRA will reject your income-splitting methods.

Capital Gains and Losses

If you bought 500 Microsoft shares in 1986 when it was first offered for sale and still hold the stock today, you would have made an enormous profit. In fact, you would be a multimillionaire on paper. If you sold your Microsoft stock today, you would have an enormous tax bill to pay on your capital gains. The moral of this tale: always remember that not all your capital gains belong to you; the taxman owns a share.

An important means of reducing the capital gains tax you pay is to time the sale of investments for a profit to occur in tax years where these profits can be offset by capital losses from selling unsuccessful investments. Currently, Canadian tax rules allow taxpayers to carry capital tax losses back 3 years and carry them forward indefinitely.

Tax Laws Evolve

Tax law is not static. Anyone who does his/her own income tax return knows that factors such as tax deductions and marginal tax rates vary from year to year. Occasionally, there is a major change in income tax law. For example, in 1971, the Canadian government undertook a major overhaul of the tax system, which included a new tax on capital gains.

> The thinking investor must pay attention to changes in tax laws.

Corporate tax law also changes. For example, on October 31, 2006, the Minister of Finance announced a new distribution tax on distributions from publicly traded income trusts and limited partnerships. The following day, the Toronto Stock Exchange (TSX) income trust index lost 12% of its value. What a Halloween prank on investors!

The thinking investor must pay attention to changes in tax laws. New laws can have an impact on the value of an investment and on investment decisions.

Tax Shelters

Tax shelters, as defined by the *Income Tax Act*, are certain types of investments that allow the investor to claim deductions or receive benefits equal to or in excess of the original investment within 4 years of its purchase. The investments for which tax shelter treatment is applicable are high risk and are generally not suitable for the average investor. If you do plan to buy such an investment, conduct a very thorough due diligence investigation before buying.

Taxes and Investing Outside Canada

U.S. Estate Taxes

Believe it or not, U.S. situated assets (e.g., Florida condo, U.S. stocks) of Canadian residents who are not U.S. citizens could be subject to U.S. estate taxes. For Canadians who are not U.S. citizens, there is an automatic U.S. estate tax exemption for the first $60,000 of U.S. assets. A larger tax credit may be available. This tax credit is calculated as follows:

> % total estate x U.S. citizen estate tax credit
> in U.S. assets

The U.S. tax credit is $780,800 for 2007 and 2008.

There are ways to reduce this foreign tax grab. You may be able to claim a foreign tax credit on your Canadian tax return for U.S. estate tax paid on U.S. assets. By investing in Canadian mutual funds or Exchange-Traded Funds (ETFs), which invest in U.S. assets, you can gain exposure to the U.S. market without actually owning U.S. assets.

If you think that your estate could be subject to the U.S. estate tax, consult a tax expert regarding foreign tax credits and strategies for reducing this foreign tax grab.

Foreign Withholding Taxes

Canadians can generally claim a Canadian income tax credit for the tax withheld by a foreign country on the dividends and other distributions paid by a company based in that country. Any tax withheld should appear on the annual income tax slips issued by the company holding your investment account.

Distributions a Canadian resident receives from owning U.S. stocks are subject to a 15% U.S. withholding tax. Financial services companies deduct the 15% before sending out distributions unless a client provides them with a completed U.S. Internal Revenue Service Form W-8EN.

When filing your annual tax return, make sure to report all withholding taxes on distributions from your investments and take advantage of any foreign tax credits CRA allows.

Inflation

Inflation is the general increase in the price of goods and services over time. Former U.S. President Gerald Ford once declared that inflation was public enemy number one. It could well be investor enemy number one too, because it is so insidious. Inflation reduces the purchasing power of money and hence its real value. If the return rate on your investments is less than the rate of inflation, you are losing real value over time – that is, you are essentially losing money not making it.

You can estimate the after-inflation return rate (called the real return rate) of an investment by subtracting the rate of increase in the Consumer Price Index (CPI)[2] from your expected return rate. For example, if you invest in a Guaranteed Investment Certificate (GIC) that pays 4% and the CPI is increasing at an annual rate of 2.2%, your real return would be 1.8%.

The exact opposite of inflation is deflation, the general decrease in the price of goods and services over time. Deflation increases the purchasing power of your money, a bonus for investors.

---

[2] Statistics Canada's standardized measure of the cost of living in Canada. Check their web site for the latest figures.

Deflation has not been seen in Canada for many years. The Canadian economy has been and is inflationary. Consequently, it is important to factor inflation into your investment plans, particularly when setting long-term goals such as retirement savings. To illustrate the impact of inflation on purchasing power, here is a sobering statistic:

> According to the Bank of Canada inflation calculator,
> <www.bankofcanada.ca/en/rates/inflation_calc.html>
> a basket of goods and services that cost $100 in 1977,
> costs $330.38 in 2007.

Remember to account for inflation when you develop your investment plan!

Part IV

The Straight Goods on Specific Investment Choices

12

Fixed Income Investing

A large income is the best recipe for happiness I ever heard of.

Jane Austen

I first started to save money when I was in public school as part of a program with the Bank of Nova Scotia. I brought my nickels and dimes to school and put them in a special envelope that was sent to the local bank for deposit. I was the proud owner of a bank passbook that recorded my meagre savings and interest too!

Like me, you probably started your investing career with a savings account. Such accounts are the simplest form of what is known as fixed income investing. This category also includes treasury bills, Guaranteed Investment Certificates (GICs) and bonds. This chapter acquaints you with the various fixed income investments available to individual investors.

The fixed income portion of your portfolio provides an ongoing positive income stream and reduces the overall risk in the portfolio. You pay for these attributes with return rates that are relatively low compared to those of stocks.

Cash and Cash Equivalents

Cash forms part of the low-risk portion of your portfolio. You should keep a certain amount of cash or cash equivalents on hand in order to purchase an investment when it becomes available at the right price. The main choices for the cash/cash equivalent allocation of a portfolio are outlined in this section.

Canada Savings Bonds and Provincial Savings Bonds

Canada Savings Bonds (CSB) are not really bonds as traditionally defined (such bonds are discussed in the section entitled Bonds). Rather, they are a financial product that the Government of Canada sells to individual Canadians with the stated goal of helping them reach their savings and investment goals. You can buy them in small amounts (multiples of $100) directly from the government, financial institutions or your financial advisor. Payroll savings plan CSB purchases may be available where you work.

Keep a certain amount of cash or cash equivalents on hand in order to purchase an investment when it becomes available at the right price.

The basic CSB provides a fixed return, is guaranteed by the government and offers the option of redemption at almost any time. The Canada Premium Bond offers a slightly higher interest rate, but can only be redeemed annually on the anniversary of the issue date and during the 30 days thereafter. The interest rates on CSBs are relatively low, usually less than the 1-year GIC rates offered by banks.

Some provinces have offered or, have offered in the past, savings bonds similar to CSBs. Ontario currently offers Ontario residents, corporations and associations three types of savings bonds: Variable-Rate Bonds, Step-Up Bonds and Fixed-Rate Bonds. The fixed rate is redeemable at maturity whereas the Step-Up and Variable-Rate bonds can be redeemed every 6 months, on June 21 and December 21 and for the following 14 days. To find out if the province where you live is currently offering savings bonds, google the name of your province and the words "savings bonds" and review the search results.

Like CSBs, provincial savings bonds are available in small denominations directly from the issuing government, financial institutions or your financial advisor.

The interest rates on government savings bonds are generally low compared to the other cash options described below – you pay for the very low risk.

Guaranteed Investment Certificates

A Guaranteed Investment Certificate (GIC) is an investment that offers a guaranteed rate of return over a fixed period of time. GICs are usually available for terms from 30 days up to 5 years. Banks and trust companies are the major issuers.

Banks are always inventing new products to market, so there are several variations available on the GIC theme.

- Escalating rate GICs offer rates that increase each year until maturity.
- Cashable GICs allow you to cash out before maturity. Naturally, you pay for the privilege with return rates that are lower than the non-redeemable version.
- Index-linked GICs guarantee the return of your original investment and offer a return rate that is linked to the performance of a specific stock market index such as the TSX 60.

GICs issued by Canadian financial institutions are low risk and can be used as part of the cash or bond asset allocation of your portfolio. I think that index-linked products should generally be avoided because they could yield low to zero return rates if the stock market performs poorly.

Money Market Mutual Funds

A money market mutual fund is a mutual fund that invests in short-term, low-risk, investments such as Treasury Bills (T-bills), certificates of deposits and commercial paper of companies. The rate of return is close to short-term interest rates minus the fund's management expenses. You buy and sell these like other mutual funds.

Money market mutual funds are an option for parking cash on a short-term basis. Make sure there are no sales transaction fees, even for short holding periods.

Savings Accounts

Savings accounts at the large Canadian banks generally pay paltry interest rates. For some of the best interest rates on cash, sign up for the high interest savings accounts offered by:

- smaller Canadian banks, such as ING bank, ICICI Bank, President's Choice Financial and Manulife Bank;
- some stockbrokers and mutual fund companies, such as eTrade and Altamira or
- credit unions, such as Steinbach Credit Union and Outlook Financial in Manitoba.

Check out the interest rate comparison charts in your local newspaper to find the organization offering the best current rates in your area. These businesses usually offer higher interest rates on savings accounts than the big banks offer on 1- or 2-year GICs.

High interest savings accounts are another place to stash your cash short term. Remember that interest rates on savings accounts can change at any time. If you want an assured return over a specific time period, consider a GIC.

Treasury or T-Bills

Treasury Bills are short-term debt obligations issued by a government at a discount to par value and repaid at par on maturity. They are considered cash equivalents when issued by reputable governments such as Canada, U.S. or United Kingdom. T-bills are yet another place to park cash on a short-term basis. These fixed income investments are available from stockbrokers.

Comparative Interest Rates for Cash/Cash Equivalents

The table in Figure 12.1 sets out the interest rates offered on a $1000 investment by various financial institutions at a particular point in time. As interest rates change frequently, view the numbers as relative only.

Figure 12.1

Comparative Interest Rates for Cash/Cash Equivalents

Type of Investment	Interest Rate (%)
Big Bank* savings account	0.05-4.00
Savings account (smaller banks, some credit unions)	0.15-4.50
Canada Savings Bond, cashable	3.10
Canada Premium Bond, 3 year compound	3.24
Ontario savings bond, 1 year fixed rate	4.75
90 day T-bill	3.65
Big Bank 1 year GIC	3.25
Smaller Bank 1 year GIC	4.50-4.80
Bank money market fund (1 year return)	3.18-4.39

*Royal Bank, TD Bank, CIBC, Bank of Montreal, Scotiabank.

Bonds

A bond is a debt instrument that is issued by an institution, usually a government, utility or corporation.
The bond is a way for these organizations to borrow
money for operational purposes such as buying new
equipment, paying off existing higher interest debt,
paying for an acquisition, etc. The bond issuer agrees
to pay fixed amounts of interest, called coupons, periodically to the bond buyer and repay the amount borrowed (the principal) on a specific future date (maturity).

> Bonds are a way for organizations to borrow money for operational purposes, such as buying new equipment.

The face value of a bond is called "par value". The term of a
bond is from 1 to 30 years or longer. Published information is
most often available for 5-, 10- and 30-year bonds. Canadian and
U.S. bonds can be purchased through Canadian brokerage firms.
Bonds from other countries may also be available. There are even
bonds of Canadian issuers denominated in U.S. dollars, Euros
and Swiss francs.

Bonds are considered safer than stocks because bondholders
have a greater claim than stockholders on the bond issuer's assets
if the issuer goes bankrupt. However, this doesn't mean you will
get all your money back if the issuer goes into bankruptcy.

Bonds come with various attributes; the most popular ones are outlined below.

- Zero coupon bonds, also called stripped bonds, are bonds that do not pay interest because the coupons have been stripped from the bond. They are bought for less than the principal and the full principal is paid at maturity. The difference between the current price and the full price is the profit. I have found that the yield on stripped bonds is lower than the equivalent regular bond. Even though no interest is paid, income tax must be paid every year on the interest that would be generated by these bonds. Given these characteristics, zero coupon bonds are best held in an RRSP.
- Real return bonds provide an inflation/deflation adjusted investment return. This is accomplished by multiplying the bond price and the coupon payments by an index ratio that adjusts for changes to the Consumer Price Index (CPI) since the bond was issued. The return on real return bonds goes up in times of inflation, but decreases if deflation occurs. Real return bonds are offered by the government of Canada and some provinces and generally have maturity dates of 15 years or longer. These bonds are an excellent choice for the fixed income portion of RRSPs.
- Junk or high yield bonds are bonds that are not investment grade. This means they are high risk and there is a reasonable chance the bond issuer will default on the interest payments or may be unable to pay back the principal at maturity. Junk bonds may pay handsomely, but are generally not worth the risk for small investors. If you want to purchase junk bonds, I think you should limit your enthusiasm to a small holding in a junk bond fund. This way you spread the default risk among many junk bonds and improve your chances of a decent return.

Investors make money on bonds from the interest paid and from capital gains if they are able to sell the bond for more than they paid. Bond prices rise when interest rates go down because the marketplace prices existing bonds such that their total return is equivalent to the interest rate of new bonds being issued.

Bond buyers are mainly large institutional investors, such as pension funds, insurance companies and mutual funds. These organizations buy bonds by the multi-millions of dollars. Often, the best bonds are bought immediately on issue by these large investors and the individual investor has little chance to purchase them.

Ways to Invest in Bonds

Bonds can be purchased in different ways, such as:

- directly,
- through bond mutual funds and
- through bond Exchange-Traded Funds (ETFs).

The advantages and disadvantages vary depending on the bond type and the investor.

Direct Purchase of Bonds

You can buy individual bonds if you have an account with a stock-brokerage firm. Here are some guidelines for buying individual bonds.

- Determine the bond's rating, that is, the risk that the bond-holder will not be paid interest on the bond or will not get the principal back at maturity. Bonds are rated by established bond rating organizations such as Moody's Investor Services, Standard and Poor's or, the only Canadian bond rating service, Dominion Bond Rating Service, <www.dbrs.com>. The best bonds are rated AAA and the lowest grade bonds are C.
- Look for investment-grade bonds of good quality or better. These are rated BBB or higher. Bonds are the conservative, fixed income part of a portfolio, so don't risk a loss with a poor quality bond.
- Buy a mix of bonds from different organizations. Federal and provincial government bonds are generally the safest and have the highest rating. This would include bonds issued by Crown corporations and guaranteed by the government. Good quality municipal and corporate bonds should also be considered.

- For further diversification, consider investing in a small holding of foreign bonds. The easiest way to accomplish this is to buy a bond fund with significant foreign bond holdings.
- For longer investing time horizons, buying real return bonds for your portfolio protects against inflation.
- Buy bonds with staggered maturity dates, known as a bond ladder. This way, when a bond comes due you are only reinvesting a portion of your bond allocation and you reduce the risk of reinvesting at a low interest rate.
- Hold bonds to maturity to keep transaction costs low.
- Outside an RRSP, other things being equal, buy bonds that trade at a discount to par because the after tax yield should be higher (part of the profit is taxed as capital gains).

Bond Mutual Funds

Bond mutual funds provide professional management and access to many fixed income investments that the individual investor may by unable to access. A bond fund owns a variety of bonds and pays regular distributions based on the interest payments of the bonds in the fund.

Some bond funds offer better tax treatment through the use of financial tricks, such as derivatives, to effectively convert bond interest into capital gains.

You do pay for the above privileges. Bond fund management expense ratio and transaction fees eat into what is already a low return, given recent low interest rates. Due to these costs, many bond mutual fund return rates are less than the benchmark bond index to which they are compared.

Two other bond fund negatives to factor into your bond investing decision: bond funds do not guarantee the return of the amount you originally invested and the value of a bond fund will go down if interest rates rise.

Bond ETFs

A bond ETF seeks to replicate the performance of a benchmark bond index by buying an assortment of bonds in order to mirror the index. Bond ETFs pay regular distributions based on the interest payments of the bonds in the ETF. Bond ETFs are not actively managed; buying and selling is limited to keeping the fund aligned with the index. As well, bond ETFs do not pay ongoing "trailer" fees to financial advisors who keep clients in the fund, so their costs are lower than bond mutual funds.

ETFs are traded like stocks – you pay a commission when you buy or sell them. If you hold a bond ETF for the long term, these one-time costs are more than offset by their much lower management expense fees compared to bond funds, especially if you use a discount broker.

Like bond funds, bond ETFs will fluctuate with interest rates and have no guaranteed return of capital.

In Canada, you can choose from six different bond ETFs from Barclay's Global Investors Canada, <www.iSharcs.ca>:

- Short Bond Index Fund (XSB-TSX), based on the Scotia Capital Short Term Bond Index™, for exposure to government and corporate bonds with short maturities (less than 5 years);
- Canadian Bond Index Fund (XBB-TSX), based on the Scotia Capital Universe Bond Index™, for exposure to government and corporate bonds with various maturities;
- Real Return Bond Index Fund (XRB-TSX), based on the Scotia Capital Real Return Bond Index™. These government bonds offer protection against inflation and should be part of any portfolio;
- Canadian Corporate Bond Index Fund (XCB-TSX), based on the Scotia Capital All Corporate Bond Index™, for exposure to corporate bonds of various maturities;
- Canadian Government Bond Index Fund (XGB-TSX), based on the Scotia Capital All Government Bond Index™, for exposure to government bonds of various maturities and
- Canadian Long Bond Index Fund (XLB-TSX), based on Scotia Capital Long Term Bond Index™, for exposure to government and corporate bonds with longer maturities.

If you want to invest in U.S. bonds, Barclay's Global Investors iShares and Vanguard each offer ETFs based on four different U.S. bond indices.

The Bottom Line on Bonds

For individual investors, there is not a lot of upside to buying bonds individually.

- An individual bond portfolio requires ongoing maintenance. New bonds need to be found and purchased as existing bonds mature.
- Individual investors often miss out on the best quality bonds as large institutional investors quickly gobble up the best new issues.
- The sales commission is included in the bond price so the true cost of the bond is unknown.

Most individual investors are best served by buying bonds using bond ETFs.

The one real positive with direct bond purchase is that you should get your capital back when the bond matures.

I believe that, given the bond ETFs available, the high expenses of most bond funds and the aforementioned concerns with individual bond purchases, most individual investors are best served by buying bonds using bond ETFs. With this approach, a few bond ETF holdings will cover the bond portion of a portfolio.

- iShares Canadian Bond Index Fund to invest in Canadian bonds.
- iShares Real Return Bond Index Fund for Canadian government bonds with built-in inflation protection.
- A U.S. ETF based on the Lehman Brothers U.S. Aggregate Index to invest in the total U.S. investment grade bond market.

If you want to include foreign bond exposure from countries outside the U.S., consider buying a foreign bond mutual fund such as the Equitable Life Templeton Global Bond Fund or a closed-end fund trading in the U.S. such as the Templeton Global Income Fund (GIM-NYSE).

Debentures

A debenture is essentially an unsecured bond, that is, a bond without a claim on the issuer's assets if the issuer goes bankrupt.

Debentures offer higher return rates (and higher risk) than the equivalent bonds. Both governments and companies issue debentures. The issuer's credit rating is an important criterion when choosing a debenture.

Various debentures are available in the marketplace.

- Senior issues are debentures that get paid first.
- Subordinated debentures will only be paid once other corporate debts have been satisfied and hence are riskier than senior issues.
- A convertible debenture is essentially a fixed coupon, unsecured bond plus an option to convert into a fixed number of shares of the underlying stock. Companies issue convertible debentures because they can borrow money at a lower cost than with straight debentures. Evaluating the investment potential of a convertible debenture is complicated because both the bond-like and stock-like characteristics need to be considered.

Government debentures include government bonds, T-bills and CSBs. Although these investments are unsecured, they are generally low risk because governments can always print more money or raise taxes to pay back such debts.

Some well-established companies issue debentures because, given their good credit rating, they don't need to pledge company assets to borrow money. However, many corporate debentures present a higher risk than bonds. If you plan to buy a corporate debenture, make sure to first check the credit rating and understand all its attributes.

13

Investing in Stocks

If you don't know who you are, the stock market is an expensive place to find out.

Adam Smith

What is a Stock?

If you watch or read the daily news, you are likely familiar with the daily dance of the stock market – stocks went up today, the stock market crashed today, etc. But, the daily news doesn't explain what a stock is or how a stock market works. That's the purpose of this chapter.

A stock or equity represents a stake in the ownership of a corporation. Over the long run, stocks deliver higher returns than bonds or cash. Consequently, your investments will likely include stocks, either directly or through mutual funds that you own. Whether you are a do-it-yourself investor or you use a financial advisor to provide stock recommendations, you need to be able to critically analyze a potential stock investment. You must decide for yourself if a stock is the right investment for your portfolio.

Stock investing is replete with jargon so I'll begin with some definitions.

- Securities are transferable certificates that indicate ownership of financial products such as stocks, bonds, debentures, income trusts, investment contracts and options.

- A share is the basic unit of stock ownership.
- A share certificate is issued to the stockowner or shareholder to document the number of shares owned.
- An American Depositary Receipt (ADR) is a certificate that represents a U.S. dollar denominated form of share ownership in a non-U.S. company. These company shares are held on deposit by a custodian bank in the company's home country. See <www.adr.com> for more details.
- The P/E ratio, or price over earnings ratio, is a very commonly used investing ratio. It indicates how much investors will pay for a dollar of company earnings.

$$P/E = \frac{\text{current share price}}{\text{earnings per share (EPS)}}$$

A trailing P/E is based on actual EPS reported in the past year whereas a forward or projected P/E uses EPS estimates published by stock analysts.

The Stock Market

A stock market or stock exchange is a public place where stocks, bonds or other securities are traded or, more specifically, bought and sold. There are stock exchanges throughout the world. The major Canadian exchange is the Toronto Stock Exchange, known as the TSX. The TSX Venture Exchange is the venue for trading the stock of small companies. In the U.S., the New York Stock Exchange (NYSE), the National Association of Securities Dealers Automated Quotation system (NASDAQ) and the American Stock Exchange are the main stock markets.

The price of most stocks that trade on a stock exchange rise and fall every day based on supply and demand. The performance of a stock exchange is tracked using benchmark indices such as those listed in Figure 9.2.

A bull (stock) market occurs when stock prices trend upwards for a prolonged period of time. A bear (stock) market occurs when stock prices trend downwards over a prolonged period of time.

Types of Stock

Companies sell or issue stock as a means of financing their business. Various types of stocks may be offered for sale, depending on the company's business needs and what investors are willing to buy. The main types of stock are discussed in the following sections.

Common Shares

Common shares are the most frequently issued type of share. Holders of common shares have some control over the operation of the company because they elect the board of directors and vote on issues affecting the company as a whole.

In Canada, a significant number of publicly traded companies issue more than one class of common shares to allow management to control the company while owning less than a majority of its shares. Typically, these dual-class share schemes grant preferential powers to one class of shares. For example, the Shaw family of Shaw Communications Inc. holds the majority of the company's class B shares, the only shares entitled to vote. Another dual class approach is that of Teck Cominco. Each Class A voting share is entitled to 100 votes while each Class B subordinate voting share has one vote.

Large institutional investors such as the Coalition for Good Governance categorically reject the dual-class structure. They prefer the one share/one vote approach as it gives them more control over the companies in which they invest.

I think that share structure is not a critical factor for individual investors. They should choose companies based on investment quality.

Dividend Paying Stocks

Some companies pay shareholders a share of the profits. These payouts are called dividends. Dividends are declared by a company's board of directors and are usually paid quarterly in cash or as more shares in the company.

The payment of regular dividends, and especially dividends that increase over time, is usually an indicator of a well-established company with assured regular income, characteristics of particular interest to individual investors.

Preferred Shares

Preferred shares are shares issued by corporations, usually large companies like banks and major utilities. These shares are "preferred" because their dividend must be paid before any dividends are paid to holders of the common stock.

Each preferred share issue has a distinct set of features. Examples of some of these features are listed below.

- *Perpetual.* No retraction date.
- *Retractable.* Shareholders have the right to redeem their shares, that is, sell them back to the company for a specified price at some future time(s) known as the call date. Retractables are bond-like since the call date is equivalent to a bond maturity date.
- *Floating Rate.* The interest rate is linked to some established rate, such as the bank prime rate.
- *Straight Rate.* The interest rate is fixed.
- *Cumulative.* Dividends not paid accrue and must be paid in future.
- *Non-cumulative.* Missed dividends disappear.
- *Convertible.* Can be converted to common shares of the company using a specified formula. The price of these shares moves with the price of the company's common stock.

High quality preferreds can be part of a fixed income portfolio and a substitute for bonds. Canadian listed preferreds have the added bonus that their dividends, unlike bond interest, are eligible for the Canadian dividend tax credit if held in non-registered accounts.

In evaluating preferred shares, you need to consider the conditions outlined below.

- *The Features of the Preferred.* Retractable and cumulative are usually better investments; floating rate is better in a rising interest rate environment.

- *The Credit Rating of the Issuer and the Preferred Share.* Choose shares of companies with Pf-1 or Pf-2 (Dominion Bond Rating Service) or P-1 or P-2 (Standard and Poor's) to minimize the risk of default on dividend payments.
- *The Yield to Call.* This is the effective yield if the share were redeemed on the next available call date. If the shares have several call dates with different redemption values, assume that the yield to call is the worst yield you could receive, a number known as the yield to worst call.

The above information should be available from any financial services provider dealing in stocks. Some financial web sites have financial calculators for yield to call calculations. Investor newsletters, such as *The Money Reporter*, may also have this information.

High quality preferreds can be part of a fixed income portfolio and a substitute for bonds.

The market for preferred shares is not very liquid in Canada. Investors tend to buy new issues, put them in a safe place and collect the dividends. Watch for new preferred share issues and consider buying them directly from the investment firm handling the new issue. However, you may want to wait to buy the new shares until they start trading on the stock exchange as some new issues will trade below their issuing price, especially if interest rates increase after the share issue details are finalized.

Given the thin trading of preferred shares you could easily overpay when buying preferred shares on the stock market. To prevent this, buy using a limit order, a price not to be exceeded order to buy. As well, do not use large all or none preferred share orders because there may not be enough shares offered for sale to fill the entire order.

Income Trusts

An income trust is a different legal structure from a corporation and is technically not a stock. It is an investment trust that holds assets that are income producing. Investors buy a share in the ownership of an income trust by purchasing units that trade on a stock exchange.

There are three types of income trusts:

1. royalty trusts, which invest in natural resources, usually oil and gas,
2. real estate investment trusts (REITs) and
3. business trusts.

Virtually all the income generated by an income trust is distributed to the unit holders without income tax being paid at the corporate level. In an era of low return rates on fixed income investments, such regular income at interest rates well above those offered on GICs or bonds is a magnet for many investors.

Many companies converted, or contemplated converting, from stocks to income trusts, drawn by the large consumer demand and by the rivers of cash that would flow into their coffers from the initial public offering of income trust units.

On October 31, 2006, the federal government ended the income trust party. The government announced that it would levy a 31.5% tax on income trust distributions starting in 2011. Note that REITS were exempted from this tax.

I believe the government took this unpopular step because corporate conversions to trusts were destroying the government's tax revenue. Part of this loss occurred because revenue from trusts is taxed in the hands of unit holders, not the corporate entity. As a result, the Canadian government was losing the tax payable on distributions from income trust units held by foreigners. On a more philosophical note, the income trust structure is not conducive to building companies and contributing to research and development and innovation, aspects of business acumen that are badly needed in Canada.

While investors will receive 31.5% less in distributions in 2011, the government will provide investors with a 31.5% distribution tax credit (similar to the dividend tax credit). This credit will not apply to distributions in a registered plan, such as an RRSP, and foreign investors will not benefit from this Canadian tax credit.

Should individual investors buy income trusts? I am not convinced, based on a number of factors. The income trust landscape has always been a minefield. Many trusts are small and high risk. Some trusts shouldn't even be trusts given the lack of stability in their revenue streams. Several have cut distributions due to problems, such as loss of a major customer. Oil and gas trusts own reserves (oil and gas in the ground) with a depleting, finite life; what happens when the reserves run out? Some trusts issue more units whenever they need cash, reducing distributions per unit. Income trusts are also prone to obtuse accounting, so the investor is never sure if there are truly enough profits to cover costs and pay the distributions.

In light of the taxation of income trust distributions, there will be a shake out in the income trust sector with the strongest trusts surviving and the weaker trusts being bought up by bigger fish. Some trusts will convert to corporations. Picking the ones that will survive and prosper is tough.

Income trusts are a form of equity. If you buy an income trust, consider it part of the stock allocation of your portfolio and evaluate it like a stock. Given the foregoing, why not consider investing in good quality stocks (and REITs) instead of tiptoeing through the income trust minefield?

Initial Public Offering (IPO) of a Stock

When a company goes to the stock market for the first time to raise money, they sell stocks in an initial public offering (IPO). If the company is a great investment, all the IPO shares will be sold to large institutional investors and preferred customers of stockbrokers. Individual investors are only able to buy the stock once it trades on the stock exchange, likely at a much higher price, as occurred with the Tim Horton's IPO in 2005.

A 2003 Industry Canada study concluded that, in general, IPO shares suffer from abnormally poor performance over the first 3 to 5 years following the IPO.[1]

Given the foregoing, I think that individual investors should take a pass on most IPOs and wait a few years to see if the company will survive before buying the stock.

How Many Stocks Should You Own?

If you invest in stocks, you want to maximize investment returns and minimize the risk of losses. One of the key ways to do this is

[1] Cécile Carpentier, Maher Kooli and Jean-Marc Suret. *Initial Public Offerings: Status, Flaws and Dysfunctions.* (SME Financing Data Initiative, Government of Canada, 2003).

to own several stocks and reduce what is known as stock specific risk. By owning several stocks, you escape a catastrophic loss if one of your stocks runs into trouble. And you never know when trouble might strike.

Consider the case of Menu Foods Income Fund, a Canadian pet food manufacturing company that ran into problems when dogs and cats started to die as a result of eating the company's pet food. The problem was traced to chemical contamination of one of the ingredients used in manufacturing its pet food. After the company issued a recall of the suspect pet food, its stock price tumbled in just a few days from $7.40 to below $4.00. If you had owned only this one stock, in a few days you would have lost over 45% of your original investment. On the other hand, if your investments were spread equally among 15 different stocks including Menu Foods, you would have lost about 3% due to the company's problems. The moral of this tale: it's very risky to own just one stock.

> Some studies of past stock market performance have concluded that owning about 15 to 20 stocks provides the best return for the least risk.

So, how many stocks do you need to own?

There is no hard and fast rule on how many different stocks an individual investor should own. A popular rule of thumb asserts that an individual stock should represent no more than 5% of a portfolio. This would mean owning at least 20 stocks.

Some studies of past stock market performance have concluded that owning about 15 to 20 stocks provides the best return for the least risk. The studies suggest that owning more than 20 stocks doesn't provide much additional risk reduction. If you own too many stocks, you'll need to spend too much time monitoring them. Life should not be focused on monitoring stocks, it's meant for enjoying many things!

Which Stocks Should You Own?

So, you need 15 to 20 stocks for optimal returns. But which stocks?

There are two main aspects to successful stock picking:

- diversifying the stocks in a portfolio and
- selecting individual stocks.

Stock Diversification

To reduce the risk of loss and the volatility (fluctuations in value) of your stock portfolio, pick stocks that are not correlated with each other. This means owning stocks that vary by such factors as industry sector, company size, geographic location and investing style. I'll expand upon these factors in the next few pages.

Industry Sector

The globeinvestor.com web site lists some 19 main industry sectors into which stocks can be slotted, everything from fishing, mining, industrial products and pipelines to consumer products, precious metals and transportation and environmental services. That's a lot of categories to track.

For purposes of picking stocks, I think individual investors can gain sufficient diversification by grouping stocks into categories that, broadly speaking, have similar economic behaviour. I like to think in terms of five general sectors.

- Consumer products and services
- Industrial products and services
- Natural resources
- Utilities
- Financials

Company Size

Small businesses generally have more opportunity to grow bigger and faster than large businesses. If successful, their returns should be higher than those of bigger businesses. A study by Ibbotson and Sinquefield of U.S. stock market data from 1925 to 1999 bears this out: the annual compound return for big companies was 11.3% and for small companies was 12.6%.[2]

---

[2]As quoted in *Investment Reporter*, January 2007.

The risk of a small business failing is higher than for a large business. Small companies tend to thrive in a growing economy, whereas in a recession, bigger, more established companies will perform better and are more likely to survive.

To improve investment returns, you may want to include some small company stocks or mutual funds of small companies in your portfolio.

Geographic Location

We live in the global village once predicted by Marshall McLuhan. The world is witnessing unprecedented growing global integration. It is no surprise then that the performance of stock exchanges worldwide is becoming more and more correlated.

Traditionally, investors sought to reduce the volatility of their portfolios by buying foreign stocks. In today's world, I believe that investment returns are more related to specific industry sector performance than the geographic location of the company. For instance, in recent years, the growth in China's demand for copper to feed its booming industries increased prices of copper stocks worldwide.

For sufficient equity diversification, I think that investors should allocate their investments by industry sector and company size rather than by geography, however, there are a couple of caveats.

- Given the preferred tax treatment of eligible dividends of Canadian companies (see Chapter 11 on taxation), I think Canadians should focus on investments in Canadian dividend-paying stocks.
- Stocks listed on the financial markets of developing countries, so called emerging markets, are high risk/high reward investments and tend to be less correlated with Canadian and U.S. stock markets. Aggressive investors may want to invest a small portion of their portfolio in such stocks.
- If you plan to live outside Canada when you spend your investment savings (retire to a condo in Florida perhaps?), you should consider putting a good portion of your investments in the currency of the country where you plan to live.

Investing Style

Choosing stocks with different investing styles is another way to diversify your portfolio and reduce the overall risk of loss.

- Growth stocks are companies with great growth prospects. They tend to be considered expensive for what you get. High-tech stocks, such as Research in Motion, are an example.
- Value stocks are companies considered cheap to buy due to certain problems, such as U.S. tariffs imposed on Canadian lumber companies reduce demand for Canadian lumber. The buyer gambles that the company will overcome its problems.
- Top down investing involves choosing stocks based on the impact of the economic outlook on the company's business.
- Bottom up investing involves choosing stocks based on the fundamentals of a specific company.

You may also hear about momentum and day trading investing styles. These are risky styles more akin to gambling than investing and I think that most individual investors should avoid them.

I believe that successful investing is not about the economic outlook or whether a stock is a growth or value stock. Rather, the successful investor picks excellent stocks and buys them at a reasonable price.

Finding Stock Investing Ideas

Stock ideas are everywhere. The shares of the coffee shop where you buy your morning coffee could be a good investment. How about the company that makes the MP3 player hanging around the neck of every kid walking down the street? Financial advisors always have stock recommendations for clients. Some discount broker web sites provide access to stock analysts' research reports. Investor web sites, investing newsletters, newspaper articles and talking heads on business television often tout certain stocks. You may even learn about a possible stock investment from someone you know.

One of my favourite ways to identify stocks worth investigating is to look at the top ten holdings of several of the top rated mutual funds in a sector in which I want to invest. Stocks appearing in the top ten of several funds are worth investigating. Most investor web sites that follow mutual funds categorize and rank funds and list the top ten holdings.

Some investor web sites rate the quality of stocks. For example, globeinvestor has a five star stock ranking system. Some web sites offer stock filters that spit out a list of stocks meeting financial criteria you have selected.

Identifying a stock that may be a worthwhile investment is easy. The hard work is deciding if the stock really is a worthwhile investment. The following stock selector is a step-by-step guide to selecting winning stocks.

Ten Steps to Selecting Winning Stocks

1. *Find out where you can buy the stock.*
   Before spending time investigating a stock, find out where it trades. Most individual investors in Canada should stick to buying stocks that trade on Canadian and/or U.S. exchanges (I'll call these North American exchanges). There are several reasons I support this idea.
   - Most stockbrokers in Canada only offer trading on North American stock exchanges.
   - If foreign trading is available, commissions are higher and you can lose money on currency exchange.
   - Companies must meet well defined standards to list on North American stock exchanges. This includes complying with demanding accounting rules. Requirements for listing on foreign exchanges may be lower, are more difficult to obtain and may require translation.
   - Foreign companies are governed by different accounting rules and hence are more difficult to assess.
   - Canadians can invest in many established overseas companies by purchasing their American Depositary Receipts

(ADRs) on a U.S. stock exchange. Companies as diverse as Toyota, China Mobile (cell phones) and Barclay's Bank are available as ADRs.

- Mutual and Exchange-Traded Funds offer foreign stock exposure, if needed.

2. *Learn about the company and its business.*
   Famously successful investors, Warren Buffett and Peter Lynch, focus on buying a business (not a stock) and understanding what that business does. This is sage advice. You can learn a lot about a company by viewing its web site and reading its quarterly and annual reports, which public companies must produce for shareholders. Detailed information on companies may also be available from your financial services provider and at the major investing web sites such as MSN Money, Yahoo Finance and globeinvestor.com.

3. *Decide if the company has a future.*
   Buy a company with a future. If you are not convinced that the company has a bright future, pick another company to evaluate. Here are some questions to help you decide.
   - Does the product or service make sense? For example, Shoppers' Drug Mart's business makes sense to me; it sells drugs, cosmetics and all the other goods I see on the shelves in its stores.
   - Is the company a leader in its field? Leadership is a significant business advantage, especially for high technology products and services. Think Microsoft.
   - What opportunities are available to grow the business? Nokia, the Finnish cell phone company, has potentially huge new markets for its cell phones in developing countries such as China.
   - Will there be enough future demand for the product or service that the company provides? Does the company have a history of evolving to meet changing marketplace demands? IBM started selling machines to tabulate census data and over time successfully transformed itself into an information systems powerhouse.
   - Who are the company's competitors? Are there aggressive competitors? Can new competitors enter the market easily

or is there a high barrier to entry? Things such as high start up costs, proprietary technology, complex regulatory requirements and need for highly skilled labour discourage new competitors. Rogers Communications and Cogeco Cable have a built-in barrier to new competitors because it's very pricy to build the infrastructure to enter the cable business and the industry is highly regulated.

Famously successful investors, Warren Buffett and Peter Lynch, focus on buying a business (not a stock) and understanding what that business does.

- What percentage of product sales will lose patent protection in the next 5 years? Are there enough products in development to replace sales from products losing patent protection? This is an important criterion for evaluating drug companies.

4. *Find out about the company's management.*

   The quality of a company's management is key to its success. Bad management can destroy even the best of companies. Assessing the quality of management is not easy for the individual investor. Here are some tips to help you decide whether to invest or move on.

   - Companies where the CEO and CFO positions are revolving doors could have problems not disclosed to the public that, once known, would make the stock a poor investment.
   - Be cautious about buying a company if the CEO or CFO has just "quit to pursue other interests". Before investing, watch to see if other departures ensue and confirm that the next quarter's financial results are OK.
   - If a CEO/CFO resigns to join another company in what looks like a promotion, it may be a good sign (the person was so good, he/she was recruited by another company) or a bad sign (talent is bailing out of a sinking company). Watch for other senior executive departures and check financial results before buying.
   - Look for senior management that includes people who have moved up through the ranks of the company.
   - If the company is family controlled and family members, especially second or third generation, are in positions of authority, scrutinize the company extra carefully before

investing. Family members should have the qualifications and experience typically required for the positions they hold.

- Be extra diligent when assessing companies with CEOs whose social exploits are routinely reported in the media. You want companies whose management is too busy looking after the company to regularly cavort with the high society crowd.

5. *Examine the company's profits.*

Companies worth buying have growing profits. Check the company's net income and earnings per share (EPS) over the last 3 years and make sure the company had earnings. The earnings should be growing steadily, at least at the average rate of the relevant industry sector. There may be the occasional down quarter, but the trend should be up.

You can find these numbers in the statement of earnings section of the financial statements. Industry comparative data are usually available in the company profiles at major investor web sites.

6. *Examine the company's revenue sources.*

Profits are wonderful, but accountants can work all sorts of magic on financial numbers to produce a profit. To get around this, examine the sources of the company's revenue. Revenue can come from such things as product sales, licensing agreements, royalties, rent or even foreign currency transactions. It can also be a one-time item, such as selling a factory that is no longer needed.

You are looking for companies with real, ongoing revenue. One-time or non-recurring revenue items may mean that revenue targets will be difficult to meet in future quarters. Read the statement of earnings section of the company's financial statements for information on the company's revenues.

You are looking for companies with growing revenues. Examine the history of revenue growth over a long time period. Some companies have variable revenues due to the nature of their business. For example, retailers such as Canadian Tire usually have much larger revenues in the last quarter of the calendar year due to Christmas sales. Software makers may have reduced revenues near the end of a product cycle and then revenues increase when a new product is introduced. Commodity-based companies, such as Petro-Canada and West Fraser Timber, have revenues tied to the price of resources and these prices vary significantly depending on the stage of the business cycle.

7. *Find out if there is a dividend and if it is growing.*
   Historical data suggest that dividend-paying stocks offer better returns than non-dividend-paying stocks. For example, Ned Davis Research analyzed stocks in the S&P 500 and found that, on average, dividend-paying stocks returned 10% annually whereas stocks without dividends returned only 4% for the period from February 1, 1972, to the end of 2005.

   > Rosy historical data aside, dividend-paying stocks are an attractive proposition because paying regular dividends to shareholders requires profits and business discipline.

   Rosy historical data aside, dividend-paying stocks are an attractive proposition because paying regular dividends to shareholders requires profits and business discipline. Moreover, if you invest in Canadian companies offering eligible dividends, you even get a dividend tax break.

   Companies that regularly increase their dividends are most likely to be ongoing thriving businesses with decent management. All the major Canadian banks and insurance companies are in this group. These companies are a very attractive investment opportunity for the individual investor, particularly investors who need income. An increasing dividend is like getting a periodic raise.

   Fortunately, there is an easy way to discover which companies have a track record of regularly increasing dividends. These companies are included in Mergent's Dividend Achievers Indices. U.S., Canadian and international indices have been developed. See which companies are in theses indices at <www.dividendachievers.com>.

   Depending on your individual circumstances, you may want to purchase a stock that does not pay dividends because it has great growth opportunities. Always remember that dividends are an important component of the total return from a stock investment.

8. *Review the company's level of debt.*

Companies borrow money to invest in and build their businesses. So, a certain amount of debt is good. However, companies with too much debt compared to their earnings are risky. What if sales are poor due to an unforeseen event (e.g., in 2005 hurricane Katrina shut down many plants along the Gulf of Mexico) and the company doesn't earn enough money to make the payments on its debt? The lender could cause the company to go into bankruptcy.

Ideally, companies should meet the following general guidelines on acceptable corporate debt levels:

- Interest coverage $= \dfrac{\text{Earnings before interest and taxes}}{\text{Total interest charges}}$

This ratio should be greater than 3 for industrial stocks and greater than 2 for utility stocks.

- Debt/Equity Ratio $= \dfrac{\text{Total debt}}{\text{Book value of shareholders' equity}}$

This ratio should be less than 0.5 for industrial stocks and less than 1.5 for utility stocks.

- Cash flow/total debt

This ratio should be greater than 0.2 for industrial stocks and greater than 0.30 for utility stocks.

If a ratio does not meet these guidelines, it should be close to the average ratio of similar businesses.

9. *Look at how the stock fits into your overall portfolio.*

If the candidate stock has passed all the previous steps, it is likely worth buying. The next step is to look at the stocks you already own to see how the new stock would affect the diversification of your portfolio. If the new stock would overweight your portfolio in one area, such as too many natural resources stocks, put your existing stocks for that area through this stock selector to decide if one of them should be replaced with the new stock.

10. *Decide when to buy the stock.*

Once you have decided to buy a particular stock, the final step is to determine when to buy. This decision can be approached in more than one way.

- Buy as soon as the decision to invest has been made. This approach is most suitable for long-term investors based on the reasoning that, over the long run, good stocks will provide acceptable returns.
- Buy a small fixed dollar amount of the stock regularly until you have the amount you want, an approach known as dollar cost averaging. Due to transaction fees, this is usually not the best way to buy stocks.
- Consider the state of the economy and technical indicators for a stock to identify reasonable buying points. These topics are discussed in detail in Chapters 19 and 20.
- Wait for the stock to go on sale before buying. What do I mean by going on sale? A stock is on sale if its price is temporarily depressed below the stock's true value. A stock is likely to be on sale when one or more of the circumstances below come to pass.
  - There is a general stock market correction or crash. For example, the September 11, 2001, World Trade Centre attack and subsequent stock market crash resulted in many good companies being on sale.
  - The stock price drops because a company news release announces lower profits for the previous quarter due to an event with a short-term impact on the company, such as a workplace strike or a power outage, which temporarily closed a plant.
  - The current P/E (price over earnings ratio) is below the stock's historical average. The company's web site and annual report may have this information or it may be available from your financial services provider. The interactive chart section at <www.bigcharts.com> allows users to chart historical P/E ratios for U.S. listed stocks.

- The stock price is at the lower end of its 52-week trading range.
- A stock analyst downgrades the company, but the company is still fundamentally sound.

While I personally favour purchasing a stock when it goes on sale, you need to decide which stock purchase approach suits you best.

The Mechanics of Buying and Selling Stocks

The stock exchange is the place where stocks are bought and sold. It is, in essence, a giant auction house with individual stock prices going up and down during the day as demand rises and falls.

You buy and sell stocks on an exchange by placing an order with a stockbroker or transaction service provider registered to trade on the exchange where the stock you wish to buy or sell is listed. You can call in your order or, in the case of discount brokerage accounts, place buy and sell orders over the Internet.

Each stock listed on the stock exchange will have:

- a bid price – the price that potential buyers have bid for a stock and
- an ask price – the price at which current owners are willing to sell the stock.

There is usually a difference of a few cents between these two prices. This is the bid-ask spread. For stocks that are thinly traded, the spread could be much larger.

Potential buyers and sellers look at the bid-ask spread, decide if they want to buy or sell and submit an order to their broker.

Stocks are generally traded in 100 share lots called board lots. If you buy partial lots of less than 100 shares, you will pay a higher price so, try to buy stocks in board lots.

For stocks with higher daily trading volumes (over 50,000 shares) and a small bid-ask spread, you can usually trade using a *market order*. For these orders, you buy or sell the stock at the current price listed on the exchange. The price you pay (if you buy) or receive (if you sell) should be close to the ask price listed on the exchange.

If a stock has a low daily trading volume and a relatively large bid ask spread, you should use a *limit order*, an order specifying the maximum price you are willing to pay or the minimum price at which you are willing to sell a stock. Your order will only be filled if there is a buyer or seller willing to meet your price. Limit orders cost a bit more, but you avoid paying more than you want for a stock or selling for less than you want. One caution: if your limit order is only partially filled during the trading day, discount brokers may charge a new commission to fill the balance of your order on the next day.

All or none orders are orders that are only filled if the shares in the order can all be purchased or sold at the requested price. For liquid stocks, an all or none order isn't necessary. For thinly traded stocks, this type of order ensures that the entire order is filled in one day and those using a discount broker pay only one commission. It has been my experience, however, that all or none orders are less likely to be filled than a market order.

If you own a stock, you can limit your loss if the stock starts to go down in price, by placing a *stop loss order*, an order to sell the stock if it reaches the specific price in the order.

Some firms offer *trailing stop losses*, an order to sell if the stock price goes below a certain percentage of the current price. With this type of stop loss, you own the stock as long as the trend is up while limiting your losses if the stock price goes down a certain percentage.

Caution is required in using stop losses. A stock that you want to keep may be sold because its price dipped, even momentarily, to the price in your stop loss order. In a heavily falling stock market, orders are filled on a best efforts basis and your order may be filled at less than your stop price.

Buying on Margin

Some stockbrokers allow clients to borrow money from them to invest. The asset being purchased is used as collateral. This is called buying on margin.

A person who buys a security on margin believes that the security will increase in price and can be sold for a profit allowing the margin loan to be paid back.

Buying on margin is risky. It magnifies profits, but it also magnifies losses. If a stock bought on margin goes down below a certain price, the stockbroker will require the investor to provide more money or securities to maintain a certain level of equity in his/her account.

I think that buying on margin is a form of gambling, which most individual investors should avoid.

14

Mutual Funds

Most individual investors would be better off in an index mutual fund.

Peter Lynch

Overview of Mutual Funds

Like many people, I started my stock investing career by buying mutual funds without actually understanding what I was buying. So, what are mutual funds?

Mutual funds are investment products created by companies and marketed to the investing public. A mutual fund pools money from many individuals and invests it according to specific objectives. These investment objectives are outlined in the prospectus that every fund must prepare and make available to those investing in the fund.

Mutual funds are securities, not deposits, so they are not guaranteed investments like GICs. They are sold in units. The value of one unit of a fund is called the net asset value or NAV. The NAV is calculated by dividing the current market value of the fund's assets (minus its liabilities) by the number of units sold. The price of fund units fluctuates daily because the market value of the investments in the fund varies daily.

Most mutual funds are open-ended funds, meaning that the fund company can sell an unlimited number of units.

Many investors use mutual funds as their principal means of investing. They have bought the fund industry's mantra that individual investors are unable to invest successfully on their own and need professional money managers to achieve acceptable investment returns. Some financial advisors recommend only mutual funds to their clients. If you have mutual funds in your portfolio or are thinking of buying a mutual fund, this chapter is required reading.

Investors can invest in virtually any type of asset via a mutual fund. While there are over 7,000 funds and several dozen mutual fund categories listed in the <www.fundlibrary.com> database of funds available in Canada, there are really only five main types of mutual funds.

1. Cash
    • Money market
    • T-bill
2. Fixed Income
    • Bonds
    • Mortgages
3. Equity
    • Canadian equity funds
    • U.S. equity funds
    • International (no Canadian or U.S. stocks) and global (all countries) equity funds
    • Country and region funds, e.g., emerging markets, China, Asia/Pacific
    • Sector funds, e.g., financial, natural resources, science and technology, real estate
4. Balanced funds – include equity, fixed income and cash
5. Other
    • Retail venture capital, e.g., Labour Sponsored Investment Fund (LSIF)
    • Alternative trading strategies, e.g., hedge funds
    • Miscellaneous

Individual mutual funds may be further defined by investing style and specific investment type. For instance, equity mutual fund investing styles include growth, value, growth/value blend, growth at a reasonable price; some equity funds are based on the size of the companies in which they invest.

Mutual fund literature frequently illustrates the characteristics of a specific equity fund by placing the fund in the appropriate cell of what is known as a style box. For a typical style box, see Figure 14.1.

Figure 14.1
Typical Style Box

Investing Style

	Value	Blend	Growth
Large			
Medium			
Small			

(Company Size)

Bond funds have their own subdivisions. The categories are typically based on the credit quality of the bonds in the fund and the average maturity of the bonds, the length of time until the bonds are due to be repaid. For example, the bond fund categories <www.morningstar.ca> include Canadian short duration fixed income, global fixed income, Canadian long duration fixed income and high yield fixed income.

The mutual fund industry periodically rearranges and renames its mutual fund categories. See the Canadian Investment Funds Standards Committee web site, <www.cifsc.org>, for the latest version. Moreover, the terminology used does not always tell the whole story. You wouldn't know by the formal name that high yield bond funds contain bonds with poor credit quality. The term commonly used for these funds, junk bond funds, is a more apt description.

Descriptive categories are a good way to begin your fund search, but you'll need to investigate a fund thoroughly to really understand what you are buying. The section entitled Ten Steps to Selecting a Mutual Fund is a useful guide to selecting mutual funds.

Mutual Fund Fees

Mutual funds are sold with the sales pitch that you get professional money management in return for a fee. In this section, I'll
take a closer look at mutual fund fees. I think you'll be surprised
at how much you pay to own a mutual fund. In the
next section, I'll discuss the track record of mutual
funds and whether the performance of mutual funds
merits these fees.

A mutual fund creates a layer of administrative
structure between the investor and the actual investment. This administration costs money – money that is
deducted from the fund's profits before returns are paid
to investors.

Mutual fund investors pay three types of fees.

> A mutual fund
> creates a layer of
> administrative
> structure between
> the investor and the
> actual investment.
> This administration
> costs money.

- *Management Expenses.* Management fees, advisor commissions, trailer fees (annual fees to advisors whose clients own a
  fund) and fund expenses (legal, accounting, marketing, etc.) are
  charged to the fund. These fees are reported as the fund's
  Management Expense Ratio or MER. The MER is calculated as
  a percentage of the average daily value of the assets in the fund.
  MERs tend to vary by mutual fund category and are usually
  directly proportional to the fund's risk level.
- *Trading Expenses.* The costs to buy and sell the stocks, bonds
  or other assets in which the fund is invested. These are not
  included in the MER calculation.
- *Commissions.* In addition to the above fees, depending on the
  fund, investors may also pay a commission to buy or sell units
  of a fund.

The management fees plus trading expenses charged by mutual
fund companies in Canada are some of the highest in the world
according to a 2007 study of mutual fund fees in developed countries. The draft review, entitled *Mutual Fund Fees Around the
World*, was written by professors from the Georgia Institute of
Technology, the London Business School and the Harvard

Business School.[1] The study reported that the average mutual fund total expense ratio (management fees plus other expenses) for all countries studied was 1.05% whereas the average of this ratio in the U.S. was 0.81 and in Canada was 2.20%!

Unfortunately, Canadian investors cannot buy mutual funds sold in the U.S., eliminating the great selection of lower cost funds available in that country.

The sample calculation in Figure 14.2 shows how much you would pay in fees over 10 years on a $50,000 investment in a mutual fund with an MER of 2.29%: $15,417.23! That's not small change.

Why not take the time to tally up the total annual fees you pay for the funds you own? A friend of mine did this and discovered she was paying several thousands of dollars per year in fees. She decided to sell the funds and use the money saved on fees to hire an independent financial advisor and invest directly in stocks and other assets.

Figure 14.2
Impact of MER on a $50,000 investment

The Investor Education Fund web site, <www.investored.ca>, has a very informative Mutual Fund Impact Fee Calculator.

I used the calculator to estimate the total fees paid to invest $50,000 in the BMO Canadian Equity Fund over 10 years, assuming a Canadian stock market return of 8% per year. The MER for this fund is 2.29% which is about average for this class of fund.

Here is what the calculator reported:

- Profit before fees $57,946.25
- Profit after fees $36,370.58
- Total fees paid $15,417.23
- Lost Profit Potential due to fees $6,158.44

You pay a lot to own a mutual fund!

---

[1] Published in the *Social Science Research Network*, July 18, 2007 <papers.ssrn.com/sol3/papers.cfm?abstract_id=901023>.

Classes of Mutual Funds

Mutual funds are also classified according to how fees are charged to buy shares in a fund. The main classes are outlined below. Individual fund companies may have additional classes and the same fund may be available in different classes. Look for funds with the class of fee structure that works best for you.

- *Class A Fund Shares*. A front end load (commission) charge is taken off your initial investment in a Class A fund share. They usually have a lower MER than Class B funds. If you buy Class A funds using a discount broker, there is usually no commission.
- *Class B Fund Shares*. Class B fund shares charge a back end load (commission), also known as a deferred sales charge or DSC. The DSC gradually reduces to zero over a specified period, usually 7 years. I think that investors should avoid this class of funds given their higher fees and the need to hold them for a long period to avoid the DSC.
- *Class C Fund Shares*. Class C fund shares have no front-end fees and a small back-end load that is normally removed after the fund is held for a short time period.
- *Class D Fund Shares*. Class D fund shares are intended for accounts where advice is not provided, such as discount brokers. These funds have lower MERs because the fees paid to advisors are minimal. RBC Direct Investing is the pioneer of this relatively new class of funds.
- *Class F Fund Shares*. These funds are for accounts where investors pay a management fee directly to an advisor. The MER does not include compensation for advisors.
- *No-load Fund Shares*. As the name implies, no-load fund shares do not charge front- or back-end sales commissions. These are often the financial services provider's own line of mutual funds but there are some independent no load funds such as Saxon, Mclean Budden, CI Funds and Philip, Hager and North.
- *Corporate Class Fund Shares*. Corporate Class fund shares allow investors to switch their money among a family of mutual funds (owned by one company) without incurring sales fees and triggering capital gains and the associated tax liability.

Performance of Mutual Funds

Investors may be willing to pay high management fees if the managers of a mutual fund deliver outstanding investment returns. However, most mutual funds provide investment returns below the benchmark indices to which they are compared. For example, the S&P Indices Versus Active Funds (SPIVA) Scorecard reports that over the 5-year period, which ended in Q3, 2006:

- less than 10% of actively managed Canadian equity funds outperformed the S&P/TSX Composite Index,
- 47.2% of actively managed Canadian small cap funds outperformed the S&P/TSX SmallCap Index and
- about 15% of U.S. equity funds outperformed the relevant U.S. benchmark, the S&P 500 Index.

These figures raise the question: "Why not just buy the stocks in the benchmark index?"

Well, you can. The stocks of many of the well-known benchmark indices can be purchased by buying Exchange-Traded Funds or ETFs. These excellent alternatives to mutual funds are discussed in the next chapter.

Do you still need mutual funds in these days of ETFs? As with most investing, the answer is: it depends. They may be of value in your portfolio:

- to adequately diversify investments if you have a small portfolio (less than $50,000),
- to easily invest small amounts of money on an ongoing basis (a good way to pay yourself before spending),
- to invest in certain asset classes not available as ETFs on the Canadian stock exchange,
- to invest in certain asset classes that the stock market does not price efficiently, that is where the stock price does not reflect all the available information about a company. This usually occurs in the case of lesser known equities such as small companies and foreign stocks. In such situations, the diligent mutual fund manager can frequently find undervalued stocks and deliver returns superior to the benchmark index,

- to invest with a specific fund manager whom you believe can deliver superior returns and
- to invest in the U.S. and avoid the U.S. government estate tax on your worldwide assets. (See Chapter 11 for more details).

One final mutual fund issue of concern, in the case of non-RRSP accounts, is the potential for capital gains payouts and the consequent tax hit to the fund holder if the manager buys and sells stocks frequently.

If you do buy a mutual fund, always remember that mutual fund companies are selling a product and intend to make a healthy profit from the sale. Buyer beware!

Index Mutual Funds

An index mutual fund is a hybrid of a mutual fund and an ETF. It is a mutual fund that tries to match the return of a benchmark index by owning the assets that make up the index.

The main benefits of index funds over ETFs are:

- small amounts can be purchased on a regular basis as no commissions are charged to buy or sell an index fund,
- any dividends accrue immediately and
- automatic dividend reinvestment, at no cost, into more fund units, maximizing the benefit of dividend compounding.

Index fund management expenses are higher than ETFs. For example, the management expense ratio for the S&P 500 composite index ETF offered by Barclays in Canada is 0.15% while the fund version offered by TD has an MER of 0.53% and CIBC's version has an MER of 0.98%.

If you want to buy index mutual funds, TD e Series funds are likely the best deal. Sadly, these funds can only be purchased on line at TD's discount broker or Internet banking web sites. TD passes on the cost savings of Internet transactions to customers in the form of lower MERs. The e Series version of the TD S&P 500 index fund has an MER of only 0.33%.

If you plan to hold an index investment for the long haul, have a reasonable sum to invest (say $5,000 or more) and use a discount broker, an ETF is probably a better choice than an index mutual fund. For smaller sums or regular monthly purchases, an index mutual fund usually makes the most sense.

To choose an index mutual fund, use the mutual fund selection guide starting on page 113.

Segregated Mutual Funds

Segregated mutual funds, or seg funds, are actually fixed term insurance contracts only available from life insurance companies. They are similar to mutual funds, but offer:

- guaranteed return of at least 75% of the original investment when the contract ends (the term is usually 10 years). This is not a huge promise since virtually all but the riskiest mutual funds make money over 10 years,
- guaranteed value to the beneficiary if you die during the contract,
- creditor protection under provincial insurance legislation,
- the option to lock in gains and reset the contract (for a new 10-year period) and
- avoidance of estate taxes and probate fees.

These features add 0.5% or more to the MER compared to that of the equivalent ordinary fund.

Seg funds are not for everyone. In fact, most investors don't need their special features. They may be useful for estate planning purposes and for entrepreneurs and small business owners who want to protect their retirement or other savings against possible creditors.

Labour Sponsored Investment Funds (LSIFs)

Labour Sponsored Investment Funds (LSIF) are corporations that invest in promising small and micro-cap Canadian companies. These are venture capital funds and they are high risk.

The tax treatment of qualifying LSIFs funds is very tempting.

- The federal Government offers a 15% tax credit on fund purchases of up to $5,000 each year.
- Most provincial governments offer a 15% tax credit.
- The Ontario government gives its citizens a 5% Ontario tax credit for research-oriented LSIFs.

Investors have traditionally bought these funds for the generous tax credits. This is the wrong reason to invest. Investment decisions must be based on the merit of the investment itself. Any associated tax relief should be considered a fortuitous bonus.

I think that LSIFs are usually a poor investment.

- These funds are high risk investing, not something most individual investors should even contemplate.
- The performance of these funds as a group has been terrible. To quote a CBC news item: "Of the 10 biggest (LSIF) funds, nine have a five-year history. All nine lost money over the five years ending May 31, 2005. Over the last year, only one of the 'big 10' has made money."
- Management fees are extremely high. To quote the same CBC item: "The average Canadian equity mutual fund has a management-expense ratio (MER) of about 2.5 per cent per year. Management-expense ratios at labour-sponsored funds typically run at four to five per cent." And you thought regular mutual fund fees were high!
- If the LSIF is redeemed within 8 years, the tax you avoided paying due to the tax credits must be repaid to the government.

Sad to say, I was once enticed by the tax advantages to buy an LSIF, which invested in medical research companies. The investment has steadily declined in value from the day I bought it and is now worth around half the price I paid. I am counting the days until I can sell this loser without having to go through the hassle of returning the tax I avoided. Learn from my mistake. Do not buy an LSIF just for the tax advantages. Buy it on its investment merits.

Closed-End Funds

Closed-end funds are mutual funds that issue a set number of shares. To buy these funds after the initial offering of shares, you must buy the shares on a stock exchange.

The average investor is not familiar with closed-end funds: financial advisors rarely recommend these funds because they do not pay trailer fees to advisors.

Closed-end funds have a number of attractive features.

- Closed-end fund managers have a stable pool of capital to invest. Unlike open-end fund managers, they never have to sell stocks they want to keep in order to fund shareholder redemptions. Consequently, returns for these funds should be better than for similar open-end funds.

> Financial advisors rarely recommend closed-end funds because they do not pay trailer fees to advisors.

- Because these funds trade on a stock exchange, Canadian investors can buy U.S.-based closed-end funds. By contrast, it is extremely difficult for Canadian investors to purchase open-end funds sold in the United States. U.S. closed-end funds offer broader product selection (over 600 funds) and lower MERs than Canadian fund offerings. For example, there are funds specializing in U.S. state and municipal bonds and over 80 funds each composed of the stocks of a single-country.
- Management expense ratios are often lower than open-end funds with similar investment mandates because trailer fees are usually not paid to advisors.
- Because the share price of closed-end funds is set on the stock market by supply and demand, you can sometimes buy a fund for less than its net asset value. This is like buying the fund on sale. Note that some closed-end funds normally trade below their net asset value.

    Fixed income funds trading below net asset value are particularly attractive because they pay out the income from the underlying fixed income assets regardless of the current market price. They effectively deliver a higher return rate than an equivalent open-end bond fund.

Here are a few caveats regarding closed-end funds.

- Many Canadian closed-end funds are structured as income trusts and could be impacted by the forthcoming Canadian tax on income trust distributions.
- Closed-end funds are thinly traded and may not be readily bought and sold.
- Closed-end funds can borrow money to invest, which adds to their risk.
- Some closed-end funds use short selling or other more exotic investing strategies. These strategies create the potential to make bigger returns or bigger losses than funds without this mandate.

Before investing in a closed-end fund, as with any investment, you need to do your homework and understand what you are buying.

The Closed-End Fund Association in the U.S., <www.closed endfunds.com>, is a helpful source of information on closed-end funds listed in the U.S. and some Canadian listed funds as well.

Unfortunately, there isn't a lot of good comparative information available for Canadian closed-end funds. The Globe Fund web site, <www.globefund.com>, does maintain a list of Canadian closed-end funds and basic information on the listed funds.

Closed-end funds are most useful if there is a limited choice in Canada of the assets you wish to purchase. For example, if you want to invest in the stocks of India, there is only one mutual fund (open-end) available in Canada that invests purely in Indian stocks. It is the Excel India Fund and it has a MER of 3.40% and a 5-year return rate of 35.04%. For more choice, you could consider the India Fund, Inc., a U.S. closed-end fund trading on the New York Stock Exchange. It has a MER of 1.49% and a 5-year return rate of 44.39% (data as of July 31, 2007).

If you decide to invest in a closed-end fund, use the Ten Steps to Selecting a Mutual Fund to help you choose a fund. Note that new closed-end funds include the fees that must be paid to the underwriter and consequently the price usually drops once the fund starts trading on the stock exchange. When you buy these funds, to avoid overpaying, it's a good idea to specify the price you are willing to pay because many closed-end funds are thinly traded and the difference between the bid and ask price could be large.

Ten Steps to Selecting a Mutual Fund

1. *Decide on the class of mutual fund that fits your investment objectives.* Use the screening tools at a mutual fund oriented web site to identify a short list of candidate funds within a chosen class. A screen for what the web site considers the highest ranked funds in the class is a good way to generate this list. Web sites that may be useful for this step include:
   * <www.fundlibrary.com>,
   * <www.morningstar.ca>,
   * <www.globefund.com> and
   * your financial services provider's web site.

2. *Get acquainted with the candidate funds.* Peruse the web site of the fund companies and review the prospectus for each fund. Confirm that the fund objectives meet your needs. Review the list of investments in the fund. Does it contain the assets you want to buy? A fund name does not necessarily reflect what is inside the fund. For example, in the summer of 2007 many investors were surprised to discover that some money market funds that they thought held safe, cash equivalent investments actually owned a higher risk investment, asset-backed commercial paper.

3. *Check the past performance of the candidate funds.* Past performance is no guarantee of future performance but it is an indicator. Choose funds that have at least a 3-year performance history and have consistently performed in the upper quartile of the fund's asset class, but be leery of buying last year's hottest funds. They usually do not perform well the following year because the great performance attracts more new money than the fund manager is able to invest in a way that produces the same hot returns.

4. *Examine the fund manager.* Is the manager a seasoned professional? Is he/she responsible for the past performance of the

fund? Does the manager invest his/her own money in the fund? Does the manager use a fund advisor? Think twice before buying a fund if the manager does not have a track record of successful fund management of at least 5 years with the fund in question or a similar fund.

5. *Consider the administrative costs of the fund.* Where feasible, choose a fund with a high minimum investment. This means less administrative costs per client account and more money for profits for you. Other things being equal, choose a fund with the lowest MER and operating expenses. Canadian fund companies usually offering the lowest fees include Bisset, Chou, Mawer, Mclean Budden, Philip, Hager & North, Saxon and Steadyhand.

6. *Look at the total fund size.* I think that it's best to avoid funds so large that the manager will have trouble finding enough good investments to profitably deploy all the money in the fund. This is a real possibility for more specialized funds, such as Canadian small cap stocks.

7. *Find out about any special policies that the fund company has in place.* Some of these policies can be a hindrance. For example, most funds have minimum holding periods to avoid redemption charges. Others are useful such as the ability to move money between funds within a fund family without triggering capital gains or charging additional sales fees.

8. *Pick funds with the lowest or no sales commission, other things being equal.* Here are some useful commission avoidance strategies.
   • Choose funds without deferred sales charges (DSC). The DSC is a commission that reduces over time to zero if you keep the fund for a long time, usually 7 years. DSCs encourage poor investment decisions: investors keep dud funds longer than they should to avoid paying the DSC.
   • Buy no load funds, that is, funds without sales commissions.

- Negotiate the commission with your financial advisor. Your advisor will still get paid: most fund companies pay an annual trailer fee as long as you own the fund.
- If you pay your financial advisor an annual fee for service, ask for F class mutual funds to avoid paying your advisor twice. F class funds have lower MERs because they do not pay ongoing advisor compensation fees.
- Use a discount broker. They usually do not charge commissions. Discount brokers do not provide advice, so ask for F class mutual funds to avoid paying advisor compensation fees.

9. *Decide the price you want to pay and when you want to buy the fund.* Choosing when to buy a mutual fund is similar to deciding when to buy a stock as discussed on page 97. With funds though, I think it's best to avoid making a lump-sum investment near the end of a calendar year if a fund has made large capital gains during the year. By waiting until January, you avoid paying income tax on capital gains you did not receive.

10. *Consider the idea that sometimes your best investment may not be a mutual fund, but rather a mutual fund company stock.*

The Mechanics of Buying and Selling Mutual Funds

Mutual funds are bought and sold in units. To buy a mutual fund, you tell your financial services provider the name of the fund and either the number of units you want to buy or how much money you want to invest. If you specify the amount you want to invest, the provider will calculate the number of units you can purchase. To sell a mutual fund, you specify the number of units or approximate dollar value you want to sell.

The unit price you pay or receive is the price at the fund valuation or cut-off time. This is usually the stock market closing time on the day your order is submitted.

Some firms offer mutual fund purchases using a regular investment plan that automatically transfers a set sum of money from your bank account to your investment account and purchases units of a designated fund or funds.

Closed-end mutual funds are available as shares. Buying and selling these funds is similar to trading stocks (see The Mechanics of Buying and Selling Stocks in Chapter 13).

15

Exchange-Traded Funds

But we are on the verge of a revolution: New research demonstrates that it is possible to construct broad-based indexes offering investors better returns and lower volatility than capitalization-weighted indexes.

Jeremy Siegel

Overview of Exchange-Traded Funds

Exchange-traded funds or ETFs are quite a different cat from mutual funds. These securities seek to track the performance of a specific benchmark index by buying and holding the assets that make up the target index.

There are over 35 ETFs listed on the Toronto Stock Exchange (TSX) and over 350 ETFs listed in the United States. New ETFs appear regularly.

For those who invest using funds, here are several reasons to buy ETFs instead of mutual funds:

- better investment performance than most mutual funds,
- easy diversification and asset allocation, even for relatively small portfolios,
- cheaper to own than mutual funds (management expense ratios (MERs) and trading expenses are lower),

- fewer capital gains distributions than mutual funds, so less tax to pay (fund managers must sometimes sell stock to fund redemptions and hence crystallize capital gains) and
- easy to buy and sell: ETFs are listed on stock exchanges and can be bought and sold like stocks.

There are a few downsides to ETFs:

- a commission is paid to buy or sell an ETF,
- dividends may not be paid out as frequently as a mutual fund or stock, so the benefit of dividend compounding is less than for these latter investments,
- some ETFs do not offer automatic dividend reinvestment; you need to invest the dividends yourself (and pay a commission to do so) and
- index ETFs are slaves to the index they track. This can have unexpected consequences for ETF returns. For example, if a company that is a large component of a stock index falls precipitously in value, the index will fall significantly along with it. To illustrate: when Nortel Networks, a major component of the TSX at the time, crashed 25.5% on October 25, 2000, the TSX benchmark index plunged 8.12%.

The selection of ETFs now available in Canada is broad enough to allow investors to construct a reasonably diversified portfolio using only ETFs. For example, Barclay's Canada, the biggest supplier of ETFs in Canada, <www.iShares.ca>, offers iShares (their proprietary name for ETFs) for a range of asset classes and sectors including:

- six different bond indices,
- the gold, energy, financial, materials and technology sectors
- dividend paying stocks, REITs, income trusts, the Jantzi Social Index,
- large, medium and small cap Canadian stock indices,
- two investment styles (growth and value) and
- two international indices, the U.S. S&P 500 Index and the MSCI Europe Australasia and Far East Index.

One of the newest arrivals on the ETF block in Canada is the Claymore group, www.claymoreinvestments.ca. Most Claymore ETFs are based on indices constructed using stock fundamental factors such as dividends paid and total sales as opposed to the traditional market capitalization technique. Claymore has a limited selection of ETFs but offers some unique indices: Canadian Dividend and Income Achievers, Canadian Preferred Shares, BRIC (Brazil, Russia, India and China), Japan and Oil Sands.

> The selection of ETFs now available in Canada is broad enough to allow investors to construct a reasonably diversified portfolio using only ETFs.

For the broadest choice of ETFs, Canadians must look south. Unlike mutual funds listed in the U.S., American ETFs are available to Canadian investors through purchase on a U.S. stock exchange. The chart in Figure 15.1, at the end of this chapter, summarizes the main ETF families available in the U.S.

Like many good investment ideas, ETFs are subject to excess. In 2006 alone, U.S. fund companies issued some 155 new ETFs according to Boston consultancy Financial Research Corporation. What was once a simple idea is now a panoply of funds based on ever more exotic indices. Some of the indices now being used, such as the Mergent High Growth Rate Dividend Achievers Index of U.S. listed companies that regularly increase their dividends, are excellent innovations in my opinion. Others, such as The Palisades Water Index of U.S. companies engaged in the global water industry, are of more questionable value. Of further concern, along with ETFs built on these more exotic indices come higher management fees and consequently lower profits for the ETF investor.

Like all other investments, tread very carefully when choosing ETFs. The selection guide in the next section will help you pick the right ETF for your circumstances.

Seven Steps to Selecting an Exchange-Traded Fund

1. *Decide on the type of assets you wish to buy and identify candidate ETFs that meet your investment objectives.* The web sites of the two major Canadian ETF suppliers, iShares and Claymore, and the ETF Centre at globeinvestor.com are the main resources for this step.

   For U.S. ETFs, begin your search at the ETF area of <www.morningstar.com> and at <www.vanguard.com>, the web site of Vanguard, a leading American ETF company that offers a wide choice of ETFs and the lowest fees in the industry.

2. *Get acquainted with the candidate ETFs.* Peruse the web site of the companies issuing each fund and review the fund prospectus. Confirm that the ETF's objectives meet your needs. Find out how long the ETF has been in existence. Look for ETFs that are at least 3 years old.

3. *Review the benchmark index on which each ETF is based and confirm that the index contains the assets you want to own.* Review how the index is constructed and decide if the index methodology makes sense to you.

4. *Review the past performance of the funds.* ETF returns should be close to the return of the index it replicates minus fund expenses. The tracking error of an ETF will indicate how closely the ETF mirrors its benchmark.

5. *For each candidate ETF, find out how long the manager has been managing the fund and if he/she is responsible for the past performance.* A manager should have a successful track record of managing ETFs for at least 3 years. Look for specific ETF management experience because managing an ETF

requires different skills than managing a mutual fund. Satisfy yourself that the manager is skilled at keeping the ETF aligned with the assets in its reference index.

6. *Review the cost to own the ETFs.* Other things being equal, choose the ETF with the lowest MER.

7. *Decide on the price you want to pay and when you want to buy.* Choosing when to buy an ETF is similar to deciding when to buy a stock as discussed on page 97. The Premium/Discount number for the ETF as listed at the ETF company web site should also be considered. This number shows the per cent the current price of the ETF varies from the value of all the assets it owns, known as the Net Asset Value (NAV). Ideally, you want to buy the ETF at or below its NAV.

The Mechanics of Buying and Selling ETFs

ETF shares are bought and sold like stocks. For the mechanics of buying and selling ETFs see the applicable section in Chapter 13, Investing in Stocks.

Figure 15.1

Summary of the Main U.S. Exchange-Traded Fund Offerings

Product Name	Description of Product(s) Offered	Issuer and Web Site
BLDRS	Series of ETFs based on The Bank of New York ADR Indexes of non-U.S. equities	PowerShares Capital Management LLC www.powershares.com
Claymore	Range of ETFs based on various fundamental value indices	Claymore Securities www.claymore.com
DIAMONDs	Unit investment trust of stocks in Dow Jones Industrial Average– 30 largest U.S. companies by market capitalization	PDR Services LLC www.amex.com
HOLDRs Holding Company Depository Receipts	Fixed portfolios of 20 stocks from a specific sector, e.g., biotech, oil, software. Option to unbundle and own each component stock	Merrill Lynch www.holdrs.com
iShares	Broad range of ETFs based on market capitalization indices	Barclay's Global Investors www.iShares.com
PowerShares	Range of ETFs based on fundamental value and other indices	PowerShares Capital Management LLC www.powershares.com
QUBEs or QQQ	ETF based on NASDAQ-100 index of 100 largest companies by market capitalization on NASDAQ exchange	PowerShares Capital Management LLC www.powershares.com
SPDRs or Spiders Standard & Poor's Depository Receipts	Range of ETFs originally based on Standard & Poor's 500 Composite Index of 500 large U.S. stocks and now expanded to other indices, company size, investing style, industry sector and region	State Street Global Advisors www.ssgafunds.com
WisdomTree	Range of ETFs based on earnings- and dividend-weighted indices	WisdomTree www.wisdomtree.com
VIPERs Vanguard Index Participation Receipts	Range of ETFs based on both market capitalization and fundamental value techniques	Vanguard www.vanguard.com

16

Real Estate, Commodities and Collectibles

The secret of success is to know something nobody else knows.

Aristotle Onassis

Most of the investing information available in the marketplace focuses on three major asset classes: stocks, bonds and cash. However, there are other, lesser known asset classes in which you can invest. In this chapter, I discuss three of these other asset classes: real estate, commodities and collectibles.

Real Estate

Most investors should count real estate among their investments. While real estate is land and buildings, investors don't necessarily need to own the land and buildings directly to invest in this asset class. So, what are the options for investing in real estate?

Before delving into real estate investing, I want to deal with the subject of home ownership and investing. If you own your home, first and foremost, consider it a place to call home. Your investment plans should not be built around the supposition that selling your home will achieve your investing goals. You always need a place to live. While your home may turn out to be a great investment, sometimes real estate does not appreciate in value and may even depreciate.

Now, to the matter at hand, investing in real estate. There are thousands of books and countless web sites devoted to telling you how to successfully invest in what I call bricks and mortar real estate – buildings and land. For example, both the Dummies and Idiot's Guide series of self-help books have titles on this topic. If you plan to invest in bricks and mortar real estate, read one of these books from cover to cover to make sure this type of investment suits you. Of particular note are the costs of owning real estate, including legal fees to arrange the purchase, property taxes, liability and property insurance, maintenance costs, etc. Real estate can also demand a fair investment of your time. If, for example, you rent one of your properties, there is ongoing work finding tenants, collecting rent, responding to complaints, etc.

> I prefer REITs because I can include real estate assets in my investment portfolio without the many obligations involved in owning bricks and mortar real estate.

Another way to invest in real estate is by buying Real Estate Investment Trusts (REITs) and the stocks of companies holding real estate. I personally prefer this approach because I am able to include real estate assets in my investment portfolio without the many obligations involved in owning bricks and mortar real estate.

If you choose to invest in REITs or real estate stocks, select these investments using the stock selection guide in Chapter 13.

Commodities

Commodities are basic marketable goods such as oil, gold and other precious metals, uranium and other basic materials, corn, coffee and other crops which are interchangeable with commodities of the same type. Nowadays, the term commodities includes foreign currencies and financial instruments and indices.

Commodities are traded on specialized commodity exchanges such as the Chicago Board of Trade. The commodity itself isn't traded; rather, a financial instrument known as a futures contract is used. This is a contract to buy or sell a defined quantity of a commodity at a certain price for delivery at a specified future date.

Trading commodities is a high-risk game. Prices can fluctuate wildly due to factors ranging from the weather to civil war to natural catastrophes and terrorist attacks.

I think that individual investors should avoid investing directly in commodities using futures contracts. If you want to invest in commodities, consider investing in the companies that produce the commodity, for example, Cameco for uranium, Husky Energy for oil or Barrick Gold for gold. Use the applicable selection guides discussed earlier in this book to select commodity stocks or a mutual fund or ETF that invests in commodity stocks.

Collectibles

I would be remiss if I didn't discuss collectibles, an asset class often hyped in books on investing. By collectibles, I mean objects that people collect with the hope of selling later for a profit. Coins, stamps, art work, depression glassware, signed photos of athletes, antique furniture, old toys, limited edition china plates, hockey cards, etc., the list of items that fall into the category of collectibles is great.

While some collectibles will appreciate in value, many do not. Furthermore, the collectibles market is extremely fickle. Demand for a certain collectible can change dramatically as categories of collectibles go in and out of fashion. I have personal experience in this regard. My son once collected action hero cards. One year these cards were the hot item all the kids bought; the next year, the card shop closed due to lack of business.

I believe that for most individual investors, collectibles should be viewed as a hobby to enjoy, not an investment. If your hobby happens to result in a profit, consider yourself lucky. If you enjoy collecting certain objects, do spend some money on your hobby, just don't consider it investing.

17

Alternative Investments – Investing or Gambling?

Sometimes your best investments are the ones you don't make.

Donald Trump

At base, there are really only a few classes of investments – cash, stocks, bonds, commodities, real estate and collectibles. Everything else is a structured product, a derivative investment that takes one or more of the above investment classes and adds various bells and whistles. These manufactured products purport to provide additional benefits to the customer compared to buying the base investment.

I talked about basic mutual funds and exchange-traded funds, the best known structured products, in earlier chapters. In this chapter I'll introduce some of the lesser known structured products that are available to individual investors.

Currency Hedging

Currency hedging is a way to reduce investment risk due to fluctuations in the exchange rate of a currency. For example, a Canadian investing in the U.S. would be interested in currency hedging to protect his/her investment against a decline in the value of the U.S. dollar compared to the Canadian dollar.

It is extremely difficult to predict the path of exchange rates;

even the professional traders get it wrong sometimes. Some exchange rate trends seem reasonably obvious based on economics, such as the decline in value of the U.S. dollar due to the massive deficit spending by the U.S. government. Once an exchange rate trend gets going, it seems to last for some time. Canadians have watched their dollar appreciate over 50% against the U.S. dollar in the last 10 years.

Currency hedging involves buying derivatives such as options and futures contracts, investments beyond the ken of the average individual investor. However, the currency risk of foreign investments can be hedged by buying mutual funds and Exchange-Traded Funds (ETFs), which are described as currency neutral or hedged. For example, TD Asset Management, RBC Asset Management, Dynamic Funds and Fidelity have currency neutral funds among their offerings. Several iShares Canada ETFs such as the CDN S&P 500 Index Fund are hedged to the Canadian dollar.

Another approach to hedging the currency risk of U.S. investments is to buy U.S. multinational companies. These companies derive a significant portion of their profits from business in countries outside the U.S. If the U.S. dollar's value falls relative to the currencies of these countries, the profit flowing in from these foreign operations increases. This reduces the impact of the U.S. currency devaluation on the company's profits.

Guaranteed Minimum Withdrawal Benefit Products

Marketers are now busily focusing on products that resonate with that major demographic segment, baby boomers nearing retirement. The latest concept is investments that include Guaranteed Minimum Withdrawal Benefits. These products are a form of variable annuity that guarantees monthly payments, no matter the current return rate of the underlying investment. They come with various restrictions such as long holding periods and extra fees for the new bells and whistles. For example, the Fidelity Monthly Income Fund with a guaranteed benefits feature has a management expense ratio (MER) of 3.4% while the Class A version of the same fund with no guaranteed benefits has a MER of 2.38%.

Be extremely cautious about purchasing investments with guaranteed withdrawal benefits. Once you buy an annuity, its irrevocable. See Chapter 23 for additional information on annuities.

Hedge Funds

Hedge funds are funds that are exempt from many of the rules and regulations governing other mutual funds. Consequently, these funds can invest in almost anything and often use highly speculative investment strategies that are unavailable to mutual funds. Hedge funds tend to be secretive about how they invest and investors often have little idea in what the fund invests. The returns of hedge funds are potentially high relative to traditional stock investments.

Like so many investing products and services, hedge funds do not share in investor losses but they do take a large share of any profits. Hedge fund investors pay the usual fund management fees and, in addition, a percentage of any profits (usually 20%).

These products traditionally had a very high minimum investment ($250,000 or more) and were once considered the exclusive purview of wealthy individuals and institutions. They are now available to many more investors through funds of hedge funds, which require a lower minimum investment and charge yet another layer of fees.

In my opinion, hedge funds are unsuitable for most individual investors given the high risk of losses, lack of transparency and the excessive fees.

Resource Limited Partnerships

Resource limited partnerships are "flow through" shares in resource companies that take advantage of the Canadian government's tax incentives to encourage investors to finance resource exploration. The gains/losses of the resource company flow through to shareholders and are taxed in their hands. These shares are very high-risk investments and are usually bought for the tax losses they generate.

I put flow through shares in the category of gambling. I think that individual investors should focus on investing, not gambling.

Mortgage Investment Corporations and Private Mortgages

A mortgage investment corporation (MIC) is a company designed specifically for lending money for mortgages. It is governed by section 130(1) of the *Income Tax Act* and pays no corporate tax. Rather, profits are paid to investors and taxed in their hands.

Investors in these corporations typically invest a specific dollar amount in a pool of mortgages. A fixed or variable return rate is offered and the rate is usually several percentage points above the returns offered by mortgage mutual funds. MIC investments qualify as RRSP contributions.

Mortgage investment corporations may use leverage (i.e., borrow moncy to invest) and are only as good as the real estate used as collateral for the mortgage and the quality of the management. So, they are riskier than traditional mortgage mutual funds.

Some provinces may allow only accredited investors (wealthy investors who can afford to lose their entire investment) to buy MICs. If this restriction exists, the MIC will require you to attest to meeting the accredited investor criteria set by the provincial securities commission in your province.

Some companies are in the business of finding investors to hold mortgages for individuals who don't qualify for mortgages from the usual sources: the big banks and credit unions. These borrowers are high risk individuals who pay high mortgage rates. Consequently, the return rate on such investments is several percentage points higher than mortgage mutual funds. The quality of the real estate used as collateral for the mortgage and the ability of the borrower to pay are critical factors in the decision to make such an investment.

Given sufficient due diligence, an investment in an MIC can provide asset diversification and an attractive investment return. Investing in a private mortgage may be suitable for some investors if the property used as collateral is sufficiently valuable. I consider these investments higher risk and allocate them to the equity or real estate portion of a portfolio.

Options

An option is a financial instrument that gives the owner the right, but not the obligation, to buy or sell a specific security or commodity at a stated price within a specified time period.

Options trading is available through stockbrokerage firms if you open an account that allows options trading. However, few individual brokers have the special license required to sell options.

Options are complicated and can be very risky. In some cases, you could lose more money than you originally invested. I believe that most individual investors should avoid trading options. If you want to get into the options game, study educational material specializing in options and find a financial advisor who is licensed to sell options and is able to clearly explain options transactions to you.

Principal-Protected Notes

Principal-protected notes are fixed income products with returns linked to the performance of a specific equity asset, such as a mutual fund, groups of stocks or a stock index. They are marketed as "have your cake and eat it too" investments – the return of the original investment is guaranteed at maturity (usually 6-10 years) and the buyer gets the juicy returns of an equity.

To achieve the advertised returns, the notes are structured into two parts, a guaranteed investment certificate and a higher risk derivative investment linked to the returns of the underlying asset. The calculation of the actual return the note provides is complicated. In addition, there may be upper limits placed on the returns offered, so if the underlying asset performance is outstanding, the note holder will only receive part of the profits.

There are substantial administrative costs associated with principal-protected notes given their complex structure. Plus, there are commissions and ongoing trailer fees to pay to advisors who sell the notes. The full extent of these fees is difficult to determine because an issuer is not required to provide a detailed information package (prospectus) when it offers these products.

Principal-protected notes have other negatives.

• The principal (your initial investment) is effectively locked up for the term of the note. It is difficult to take the money out before maturity and there may be early redemption fees to do so.
• The guarantee of return of capital only applies if the note is held to maturity.
• The returns, if any, on notes held to maturity are taxed as interest income. In contrast, if you invest directly in stocks, any increase in value is considered a capital gain and taxed at a lower rate than interest income.

I am not a fan of principal-protected notes. I think investors are better off buying basic fixed income products if they want guaranteed returns and buying stocks or an ETF for the higher returns that equities offer.

Private Equity

Private equity firms are in the business of raising money privately, that is, they do not use public stock exchanges, and then investing the capital for a handsome profit. The best known of such firms are leveraged buy out specialists. These companies typically operate by buying up all the shares in a public company and taking it private. Often, the purchase is made largely with borrowed money and the target company is used as collateral. The private equity firm overhauls the company, often laying off workers and selling profitable divisions. After extracting as much money as possible from the company, it then sells the business by issuing shares of the revamped company on a public stock exchange.

Some private equity firms, such as Fortress Investment Group LLC and Blackstone Group, now raise money by issuing shares on public stock exchanges. Talk about a contradiction in terms!

In my opinion, private equity investing is extremely risky and most individual investors should probably steer clear of this asset class.

Split Share Corporations

Split share corporations buy common shares of one or more companies (often an industry sector such as banks) and then issue two classes of shares with very different risk profiles.

- *Preferred Shares.* Preferred shares generate fixed, cumulative dividends and return the original investment at a specified date. The risk of loss of the initial investment is low and there is a steady stream of dividends.
- *Capital Shares.* The profit from these shares is variable and is based on capital gains (or losses), and any increases/decreases in the dividends paid by the common shares of the companies held. Because of the way these shares are structured, the capital gains and losses are magnified compared to the underlying stock.

Split shares usually have redemption dates. At that time, the underlying shares are sold, the preferred shareholders are paid back their original investment and the capital shareholders get what's left.

I don't think split shares are great investments for most individual investors. Like mutual funds, the split share corporation charges ongoing fees on the value of the assets. Why not consider buying a company's preferred shares directly and avoid these ongoing fees? The capital shares are risky given their ability to magnify losses.

Scotia Managed Companies is a major player in the split share corporation business. If you want more information on split share corporations, check out their web site at <www.scotiamanagedcompanies.com>.

Gambling Asset Class

Certain so-called "investments" are what I would classify as gambling. The list of "investments" I would put in this category is long and includes:

- initial public offerings, especially of fairly new companies
- penny mining stocks,
- flow through shares,

- options and futures contracts and
- any investment bought on the basis of information that cannot be confirmed, e.g., "hot tips" from friends, stocks rumoured to be taken over by another company.

Some people feel they must have gambling in their life. If you are among this group, I suggest you satisfy this need by annually allocating a small, fixed amount of your savings to what I'll call the gambling asset class. Only allocate money you can afford to lose without jeopardizing your investing goals. Set up a gambling account that is separate from your investing account.

If you choose to gamble, remember this cardinal rule: Never rob your investing account to feed your gambling account.

Summing Up Alternative Investments

The marketing departments of investment firms are always busy creating new structured products to sell. I like to call them "flavour of the month" investments. What is common to these alternative investment products are the substantial fees investors pay to the company that develops and offers the product. These fees eat into investment returns.

I believe that there is a place in the portfolios of some individual investors for shares of a quality MIC and possibly selected private mortgages. I am not so sure about the other alternative products discussed above. I personally think that sticking to sound stocks, fixed income investments, mutual funds, real estate and ETFs offers a better risk-reward proposition for most individual investors.

> Common to these alternative investment products are the substantial fees investors pay to the company that develops and offers the product – fees that eat into investment returns.

Part V

Investment Decision Making

18

When to Buy, When to Sell

No one was ever ruined by taking a profit.

Stock market adage

When to Buy

Deciding when to buy an investment should be relatively easy. The same general approach works for most investments: you do your homework, decide what to buy and how much you are willing to pay and then wait until the investment is available at your price. Of course, the devil is in the details. That's why a selection guide and when to buy advice are included for each of the asset classes discussed in Part IV: The Straight Goods on Specific Investment Choices.

When to Sell

In an ideal world, investors would buy, hold and prosper, to borrow the tag line of AIC, a well-known Canadian mutual fund company. In the real world, some investments are duds and need to be sold while others produce a fine profit and then languish or fall on hard times.

I think that figuring out when to sell an investment is the most difficult aspect of investing. In this chapter, I'll try to provide some guidelines on when to sell.

Selling Fixed Income

There should be little need to sell fixed income products. Buy good quality bonds and the Guaranteed Investment Certificates (GICs) of financial institutions who are members of a deposit insurance fund, hold them to maturity and reinvest. It's even easier with bond mutual funds and exchange-traded funds (ETFs), just buy and hold.

Investment grade government bonds and debentures should generally be held to maturity given their low risk. Corporate bonds and debentures require more attention. The health of the company issuing the debt needs to be monitored. If its business starts to decline significantly, the bond or debenture may need to be sold before maturity to avoid the risk of default on repayment of the principal.

Investments in mortgage investment corporations and private mortgages usually have specific maturity dates. Like other fixed income products, buy and hold to maturity. However, examine the corporation before reinvesting, to reassure yourself that the risk of default on interest payments and return of your capital at maturity is still acceptable.

Selling Stocks

I believe that the goal of stock investing for most individual investors should be to buy and hold good stocks for the long run. However, sometimes you do need to sell. You should consider selling a stock in the following situations.

- You need the money for a down payment on a house for example.
- You receive an attractive offer to buy the company.
- The stock becomes too large a portion of your portfolio. Sell some to reduce your holding to 5%.
- Your initial evaluation of the company was wrong. For example, you used incorrect information in your original analysis and based on the new information the stock is not a good investment.
- The company's circumstances change in a way that will have a

significant negative impact on its performance. Determining if new information is important enough to merit selling is tricky. Some situations that suggest it's time to consider selling include:

- A customer who accounts for a significant portion of a company's profit is lost and the company will have great difficulty replacing these sales.
- The CEO or CFO are fired or are charged with financial irregularities.
- Changes to government regulations have a major impact on the company's ability to make a profit.
- The economy is slowing down and the company does not perform well in a recession.
- Technical indicators (see Chapter 20) generate a sell signal.
- The stock has reached the lowest price you are willing accept. Portfolio risk can be reduced by controlling stock losses to a percentage of the purchase price. To do this, use stop loss orders, which are discussed in the next section.
- You trigger a capital loss on an underperforming stock to offset capital gains made elsewhere and reduce the income tax you pay.

A final word on selling stocks: if you pick stocks wisely, there will be few situations arising that will require a stock to be sold. Consequently, sober reflection is in order before finalizing a decision to sell. Above all, do not sell a good stock in a panic. Many of those who panicked and sold stocks after the World Trade Center attack in 2001 have lived to regret their decision.

Stop Loss Orders

Risk-adverse investors can use stop loss orders to limit their losses. A stop loss order is a standing order to sell a company's shares if the stock price falls below a specific value. Virtually all stockbrokers offer this type of order.

A stop loss order is a good idea in theory but may, in practice,

Trailing stop loss orders are the best way to use stop losses. trigger the sale of a stock you wanted to keep if the stock price hits the stop loss price, even for only a minute or two.

Unfortunately, not all stockbrokerages have the trailing stop loss capability. If you plan to use trailing stop losses, make sure that the financial services provider you hire offers them.

In my opinion, trailing stop loss orders are the best way to use stop losses. These are sell orders in which the selling price is set at a fixed percentage below the market price of a stock. So, the selling price fluctuates with the market price of the stock. This technique limits losses without limiting maximum gains. Best of all, trailing stop losses reduce the need for ongoing stock price monitoring.

Unfortunately, not all stockbrokerages have the trailing stop loss capability. If you plan to use trailing stop losses, make sure that the financial services provider you hire offers them.

Selling Mutual Funds and ETFs

Guidelines for selling mutual funds differ from those for individual stocks. The sell decision is largely focused on the fund manager, the fund company and the asset class of the fund.

Re-evaluate your ownership of a mutual fund when these situations occur.

- You need the money.
- The fund becomes too large a portion of your portfolio and you need to trim your holding to maintain the target percentage for the relevant asset class.
- The fund is underperforming relative to its peer group or the applicable benchmark. Relative performance data is available at established investor web sites such as globefund.com. A quarter or two of sub-par performance is not of real concern. Review longer term performance (at least a year) when making this assessment.
- The fund has been amalgamated with another fund. This is a red flag. Amalgamation usually occurs when a fund has performed poorly and it necessitates a complete review of the new fund.
- The fund has changed its style or objective and no longer fits your investment portfolio. For example, if a Canadian stock fund investing in large conservative companies expands its

mandate to include small companies, the fund's risk level could increase beyond acceptable levels. Also, your portfolio could be overweight in such stocks if you already own a small cap stock fund.

- The fund manager changes, particularly if the fund performance is attributed to a "rock star" manager and this person leaves.
- Fund expenses rise and are above peer group levels.
- You trigger a capital loss on an underperforming fund to offset capital gains made elsewhere and reduce the income tax you pay.
- The fund size changes significantly. This is a particular issue if the fund is a small company asset class. If the fund has too much money, it will have trouble finding enough decent small company stocks to buy.

How to Behave When the Stock Market Isn't

An intrinsic feature of the stock market is that stock prices rise and fall. If you invest in stocks, you must accept this fact. On occasion, stock prices rise or fall very quickly. For example, in the summer of 2007, the S&P/Toronto Stock Exchange Composite Index lost some 12% of its value over a three-week period. Trading in such volatile stock markets is fraught with risk.

If the stock market is taking a wild ride up or down, do not buy or sell in a panic. Instead, sit back, have a drink and remind yourself that you have an investment plan and you intend to stick to that plan. Always focus on buying investments based on the quality of the investment itself.

Selling Real Estate

I regard bricks and mortar real estate as a buy and hold investment given that such real estate is usually not liquid and there are significant costs to selling (real estate agents, legal fees, land transfer taxes, etc.).

As noted in Chapter 16, the finer details of investing in bricks and mortar real estate are beyond the scope of this book. If you plan to invest, take the time to educate yourself about the business of owning real estate, including when to sell.

If you invest in real estate via a stock or real estate investment trust, the guidelines on when to sell are the same as those outlined above for selling stocks.

19

The Economy and Investing

If all economists were laid end to end they would never reach a conclusion.

George Bernard Shaw

Historically, economic activity has grown and declined in cycles of varying length known as business or economic cycles. These cycles are recognizable in everyday life. The economy grows, businesses' profits increase, the stock market goes up, there are lots of jobs available and new businesses open up. Then, the economy starts to decline, the term recession appears in the news, unemployment rises, businesses' profits decrease, the stock market goes down and some businesses shut down.

The return rates of various industry sectors usually peak at different stages of the business cycle.

- Natural resources (energy, metals, forest products) and technology stocks tend to perform best early in the economic cycle as the manufacturing industry buys the raw inputs and equipment needed to increase production.
- Next, industrial stock performance improves as profits roll in from this increased production.
- Then, utility stocks take their turn as they profit from the increased demand for electricity, telephone services, gas, etc.
- Later in the economic cycle, employment has improved and consumer spending increases, especially on the non-essentials of life. Stocks of companies providing the finer things in life do well.

- In the late stages of the economic cycle, financial stocks do well as they reap the benefits of increased loans to businesses and consumers, more credit card spending and increased sales of mutual funds.
- When a recession sets in, the stocks of businesses supplying consumer staples, such as food, and minor indulgences, such as cigarettes and alcohol, tend to do best. After all, everyone has to eat.

While investment decisions should be based on the quality of the individual investment, it makes sense to also consider the state of the economy.

Interest rates also tend to move in cycles. Rates usually trend up when the economy is expanding. Central banks strive to manage the expansion and control inflation by raising interest rates and making money more costly to borrow in order to invest. When the economy needs a boost to grow, rates trend down making money cheap to borrow for investing.

While investment decisions should be based on the quality of the individual investment, it makes sense to also consider the state of the economy. The state of the economy is usually discernible from reports in the business media.

Here are some examples of how economic factors might affect investment decisions.

- If the economy is going into recession, you sell investments that usually perform poorly in recessionary times and switch to stocks that do well in a poor economic environment, such as utilities and consumer staples.
- If the economy is going into recession, you increase the fixed income allocation in your portfolio.
- If the economy is growing, you increase the proportion of stocks and stock-based investments in your portfolio.
- If interest rates are rising, you buy fixed income investments with short maturity dates so you can reinvest the money at higher interest rates in the near future.

20

Market Timing and Technical Analysis

Even a correct decision is wrong when it was taken too late.

Lee Iacocca

Market Timing

Is it possible to predict the direction of the stock market? Can you profit by buying and selling investments based on such predictions? In other words, to use investment industry jargon, can you time the market?

The good news is that I believe investors can improve investment returns by market timing. The bad news is, it takes a lot of skill, time and effort to be a truly successful practitioner of market timing, probably more time than most investors are willing to devote.

Despite the foregoing, I think there are two ways for investors to improve their investment returns by market timing.

1. Use economic data to assist in investment decision making, as discussed in the previous chapter on business cycles and investing.

2. Use technical analysis (as discussed in the next section) to help determine when to buy and sell an investment after you have decided what investments to buy or sell.

Technical Analysis

Technical analysis is a method of evaluating stocks and the stock market by using charts that analyze historical prices and trading volumes. Practitioners of technical analysis (and there are many) make buying and selling decisions based on what they claim their charts show. They spend little or no time analyzing the business behind the stock or the assets held in a mutual or Exchange-Traded Fund (ETF) to determine its investment quality.

I figure that if a technical analysis technique could really predict when to buy or when to sell an investment, the inventor of the technique would never tell anyone. Rather, he/she would use the technique to amass a fortune and then retire to a spectacular estate in the tropics.

While interesting patterns and trends can be identified by technical analysis, I personally believe that technical analysis is largely slicing and dicing historical data to justify investment decisions. Individual investors are better served by making investment decisions about what to buy or sell based on an understanding of fundamental information about an investment, not the wobbles in a stock chart.

While I do not place great faith in technical analysis, I believe there are a few technical analysis techniques that can improve the odds of buying or selling an investment at the optimal price. These techniques should be considered as another piece of information to help investment decision making once you have determined what to buy or sell based on your own independent analysis of the fundamentals of a particular investment.

Moving Averages

The simple moving average of a stock, ETF or mutual fund is its average price over a specified time period, usually 50 or 200 days. Using averages flattens out large price fluctuations and makes it easier to spot pricing trends. These trends can assist in timing the purchase or sale of investments. Most investment web sites have tools to graph moving averages of stocks, ETFs and mutual funds.

The following moving average techniques are some of the most popular technical analysis tools used by investment industry professionals to time investment decisions.

200-Day Moving Average Trending Up

If the 200-day moving average (price) of an investment is trending up and the current price is above this average, the price trend is up and it's considered a signal to buy.

Figure 20.1
200-Day Moving Average Trending Up

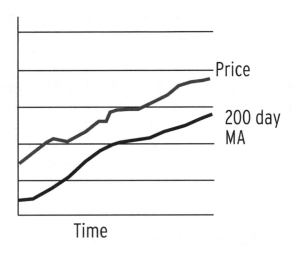

200-Day Moving Average Trending Down

If the 200-day moving average of an investment is sloping down and the current price of the investment is below this average, the price trend is down and it's considered a signal to sell.

Figure 20.2
200-Day Moving Average Trending Down

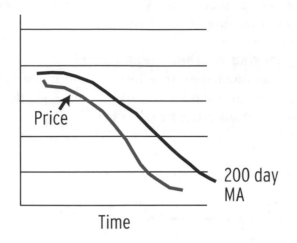

Crossover of Shorter and Longer Moving Averages

If a shorter moving average (typically 50 day) crosses a longer moving average (typically 200 day) from below, it's considered a possible buy signal. If the shorter moving average is above the longer term moving average and crosses and dips below the latter average, it could be a sell signal.

Figure 20.3
Crossover of Shorter and Longer Moving Averages

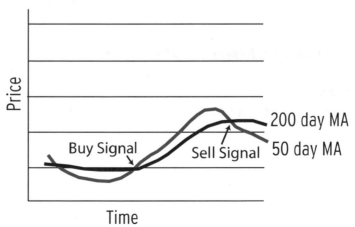

Average Trading Volume and Average Prices

Over time, stocks usually exhibit an average daily volume of shares traded and an average daily range in price. In the world of technical analysis, variations outside these averages generate buy/sell signals. Below are the most common indicators of this type.

- *A rapid increase in the daily trading volume of a stock with the price trending down.* This is a sell signal. This usually indicates that something is wrong with the stock. For example, news that a refinery fire will stop gasoline production for several weeks usually results in a flurry of selling of the shares in the company owning the refinery.
- *Sudden large increases in the volume of stock sold with a price trending up.* This is a buy signal. Again, there is usually some fundamental factor such as a rumoured takeover by another company, which causes the abnormal trading price/volume in the company's stock.

If you observe volume or price anomalies in one of the stocks you own, check out the latest information available about the company to determine if your opinion about owning the stock has changed.

> If you observe volume or price anomalies in one of the stocks you own, check out the latest information to determine if your opinion about owning the stock has changed.

Reversion to the Mean

I believe that financial ratios such as Price per Earnings (P/E), like much other data, are subject to that old statistical concept, reversion to the mean. Based on this thinking, if a stock is well above its long-term average price or P/E ratio, odds are that the price or ratio will fall toward its longer term average value. The reverse also holds: if a stock or P/E is well below its average, odds are that it will move upward toward its longer term value. Longer term is a relative concept; I usually think in terms of a time frame of at least 1 year.

The U.S. Presidential Cycle

Countless paper has been expended in the quest to identify patterns or cycles in the ups and downs of the stock market. While most resulting theories are too complicated or unreliable to mention in this book, the one theory that is reasonably simple to understand and seems to hold true is the U.S. Presidential Cycle. This theory proposes that the returns of the U.S. stock market are linked to the specific year of the 4-year term of a U.S. president.

While specific gains and losses by year depend on the years included in the study, data reported by U.S. money management firm GMO illustrate the model.[1] GMO analyzed the performance of the S&P 500 Index beginning in 1964 and found that, on average, in the first year of a President's term the Index gains 1.3%, in the second year it declines 8.4%, in the third year it rises 24.1%, and in the last year it gains 7.4%.

If you subscribe to this theory, there are key points to factor into your stock investing decisions.

- The first year of a Presidential term has the worst returns, possibly because the new regime is implementing the tough economic medicine it thinks is required to deliver on its agenda.
- Returns are usually best in the third year of a Presidential term. GMO concluded that this is due to the government stimulating the economy to increase jobs in anticipation of the election in year four. Evidently, employment moves the vote.
- Regardless of anything, the market goes up in the 15 months starting in October of the second year of a U.S. Presidential Cycle.

---

[1] Jeremy Grantham as quoted in "Inside The Mind of a Legend" by Corey Hajim *Fortune*, March 15, 2006.

Part VI

**Addressing
Investment
Related
Personal Needs**

21

Retirement and Investing

Annual income twenty pounds, annual expenditure nineteen six, result happiness. Annual income twenty pounds, annual expenditure twenty pound ought and six, result misery.

Charles Dickens, *David Copperfield*

Saving for Retirement

Every year in January and February, Canadians suffer through another season of advertisements exhorting every person in the workforce to contribute to his/her Registered Retirement Savings Plan (RRSPs). Print ads, television spots, web site pop ups, even ads on the sides of buses, implore us to top up our RRSPs. Some ads pitch the soft sell approach – talk to us we can help. Others promote the tax deduction that an RRSP provides. Still others, the most odious, suggest that if you don't contribute, you'll still be working at 80 flipping burgers in a fast food restaurant.

Do you really need to save for retirement or will the government old age benefits and your pension (if any) provide enough income for a comfortable retirement?

The Canada Pension Plan and Old Age Security provide sufficient money for only the most basic of life styles. Many employers in Canada do not have pension plans for their employees. Unless you are one of the dwindling number of Canadians whose employer offers an inflation protected, defined benefit pension plan, you will need to save for retirement and invest those savings to provide a comfortable income in your old age.

What Is the Best Way to Save for Retirement? RRSPs or Not?

The aforementioned RRSP is the federal government's way of encouraging Canadians to save for retirement. A taxpayer receives an income tax deduction (usually about 18% of the previous year's earned income) for RRSP contributions up to a maximum limit. The government is raising contribution limits over time (see Figure 21.1).

Figure 21.1
RRSP Contribution Limits for 2007-2010

Year	RRSP Contribution Limit
2007	$19,000
2008	$20,000
2009	$21,000
2010	$22,000

An RRSP is an income tax deferral tool. You get a tax deduction today and your investments grow tax-free inside the RRSP. When you take the money out of the RRSP, you pay tax on this income.

Should every Canadian have an RRSP? Not necessarily. It all depends on your individual circumstances. If a person will likely be in the same or lower tax bracket when the RRSP funds are withdrawn, an RRSP is probably a good investment. On the other hand, an RRSP contribution is of questionable value for those with income low enough that an RRSP contribution will not reduce the income tax owed.

Consider paying off debt first before contributing to an RRSP. You can save up unused RRSP contribution room and make a large RRSP contribution in the future when you have no debt.

If your employer has a group RRSP plan and matches employee RRSP contributions, I think it makes sense to participate. Your employer's contribution is like a pay raise.

If you do invest in an RRSP, consider its limitations.

- Capital gains created inside an RRSP are effectively taxed as income when withdrawn from the RRSP.
- Capital losses inside an RRSP cannot be claimed on your tax return.
- The benefit of the Canadian dividend tax credit is lost for eligible dividends inside an RRSP.
- Inside an RRSP, you do not have the advantage of timing an investment sale to minimize the tax you pay on capital gains.
- Large RRSPs, once collapsed (which is mandatory at age 71) could create an annual stream of taxable income large enough to reduce your Old Age Security pension.

Asset Types Best Suited to RRSPs

Given the above limitations, the best types of investments for an RRSP are fixed income assets like bonds and GICs.

If you do invest in stocks, it makes sense to hold your U.S. or foreign stocks in your RRSP and put your Canadian dividend paying stocks outside your RRSP so you can claim the Canadian dividend tax credit. Another reason to hold U.S. stocks in your RRSP is that U.S. source dividends are not subject to tax when held in an RRSP.

RRSP Contributions and Your Mortgage

As I noted early in this book, one of the most fundamental steps to investment success is paying off debt first. A mortgage is debt. So, in principle, I advocate paying off a mortgage as quickly as possible before contributing to an RRSP.

There is one concern with this approach. Investing all your money in a single asset, your house, does not provide asset diversification. As you now know, lack of diversification is a risky way to manage your investments.

There is a way to diversify your assets, save for retirement and pay down your mortgage debt – make an RRSP contribution and use the tax refund that the contribution provides to make a lump-sum payment on your mortgage.

To complete the above strategy, invest your RRSP in non-real estate assets. This means not holding the mortgage on your home inside your RRSP, a strategy promoted by some financial institutions. In any event, the procedure to put your mortgage in your RRSP is complicated and costly with set-up fees, legal fees, ongoing administrative fees and mortgage insurance premiums to pay.

How Much Money Do You Need to Retire?

Financial advisors may tell you that most people need to save millions of dollars before retiring. This is extremely self-serving.

> You may or may not need millions to retire: it depends on how you plan to live after you retire.

Advisors are often paid based on a percentage of assets under their care; so the more their clients save, the more money they make. In his book, *Smoke and Mirrors: Financial Myths that will Ruin Your Retirement Dreams*,[1] accountant David Tahair has made a good case that Canadians need much less money to retire than what the financial professionals recommend.

You may or may not need millions to retire: it depends on how you plan to live after you retire. Naturally, if on retirement you want to live in a large home in a major city, buy a $500,000 vacation condo in Florida and a ski chalet in Whistler as well as travel the world, you will need more money than if you retire to a simple life in a modest home in a small town.

To figure out how much money you will need to retire, you must:

- estimate your own annual personal expenses in retirement factoring in inflation over your retirement years,
- determine the annual revenue before taxes that you'll need to generate enough after-tax money to meet your expenses and
- figure out where this revenue will come from, be it company pension, RRSPs, personal savings, Canada Pension Plan, etc.

---

[1] David Tahair, *Smoke and Mirrors: Financial Myths that will Ruin Your Retirement Dreams*, 4th ed. (Self Counsel Press, 2006)

Trahair's book comes with an Excel spreadsheet that allows readers to estimate their living expenses and "The Retirement Optimizer" spreadsheet for testing spending, retirement revenue and longevity scenarios. Similar calculators are available from your financial advisor and insurance and financial companies. Such tools will help you realistically estimate how much money you'll need to retire.

How Should You Invest Your Money Once You Retire?

After retiring, you must invest your savings in a way that provides sufficient income for the rest of your life. Factoring the ups and downs in the equity portion of your retirement nest egg is critical to achieving this goal. Your financial advisor should be able to provide guidance on the appropriate asset allocation for your retirement savings based on such factors as the expected return rate of your investments, the inflation rate, the rate money is withdrawn and the number of years of withdrawals.

The following two writers offer useful insights into this subject.

* *Jim Otar*[2] has analyzed various model retirement portfolios after 10, 20 and 30 years of regular withdrawals. He calculated the optimum asset allocation (stock vs. fixed income) and asset rebalancing frequency for various expected return rates and withdrawal rates. For example, he calculated that a 60% fixed income/40% stock portfolio with the same stock returns as the Dow Jones Industrial Average and no portfolio rebalancing has a zero probability of depleting after 30 years using a 3.4% initial withdrawal rate.

---

[2] Jim Otar, *High Expectations and False Dreams, One Hundred Years of Stock Market History Applied to Retirement Planning.* (Otar and Associates, 2001).

- *Professor Moshe Milevsky*[3] presents a thought-provoking discourse on asset allocation and retirement. He concluded with the most important question to ask anyone offering you financial retirement advice: What are the odds that I will outlive my money, if I follow your suggestions? Excellent food for thought!

Options for Collapsing an RRSP

Once you reach age 71 you must shut down your RRSP. There are several choices for handling the proceeds of your RRSP with varying tax implications.

Purchase an Annuity

If you purchase an annuity, the RRSP proceeds are not taxed. The annuity provides a guaranteed income (usually for the rest of your life). Annuity payments are taxed as you receive them. There is more about Annuities in Chapter 23.

Set Up a Registered Retirement Income Fund (RRIF)

The RRSP proceeds will not be taxed if you convert the RRSP to a RRIF. A RRIF has the advantages and disadvantages of an RRSP. You can invest in various securities but all withdrawals are taxed as income. This could produce higher returns than an annuity albeit at a greater risk. A certain percentage (based on your age) of the RRIF must be withdrawn each year and reported as income for tax purposes.

Withdraw the Funds

Withdrawn money can be invested as you wish. This is generally not a good strategy as it creates a high income in one year and hence you pay income tax at a higher tax rate than you normally would.

---

[3] Moshe Milevsky,. *Money Logic, Financial Strategies for the Smart Investor.* (Stoddart Books, 1999).

Gradual Withdrawal of Funds before Age 71

This strategy is rarely mentioned, but I think it merits consideration. Depending on your age at retirement, your tax bracket and pension income (if any), the best strategy for closing down an RRSP may be to annually withdraw some money from your RRSP beginning when you retire (presumably at 65 or younger). The goal is to exhaust much of your RRSP by age 71, the mandatory date for collapsing an RRSP. Tax is paid on the withdrawals, but the tax rate should be lower than when you worked.

The advantages of this approach over a RRIF include:

- maximum flexibility in how you invest your money,
- better control of income. No mandatory RRIF withdrawals that could boost your income to a level that reduces your Old Age Security pension,
- capital gains are not taxed as income, but at the lower capital gains tax rate,
- capital losses can be claimed on income tax and
- a tax credit can be claimed for any eligible Canadian dividends.

Locked-in Retirement Savings Accounts

If an employee leaves an employer, the employee may have accrued pension benefits. If these benefits are withdrawn from the employer's registered pension plan, they must be placed in a locked-in registered retirement savings plan (LRRSP) or a locked-in retirement account (LIRA). These "locked-in" accounts are intended to provide regular income once a person retires and no money can be withdrawn prior to retirement. Provincial pension legislation defines the rules around such accounts. LRRSPs and LIRAs have many of the shortcomings of RRSPs and, given this, should be invested like RRSPs with a focus on fixed income assets like bonds and GICs.

After retirement, a LIRA or LRRSP is converted into an investment vehicle to generate ongoing retirement income. Depending on the province, this could be:

- a life annuity,
- a life income fund. This is a RRIF with restrictions on maximum withdrawals and the requirement to convert to an annuity at age 80 and
- a locked-in retirement income fund. This is a RRIF with restrictions on minimum and maximum withdrawals but no requirement to convert to an annuity at age 80.

The rules around converting LIRAs into one of these options are complicated and, as noted above, vary according to the applicable provincial pension legislation. If you have one of these accounts, consult a qualified financial professional who is an expert in LIRAs before deciding on the best option for your situation.

22

Investing for Your Children's Education

Education is the most powerful weapon which you can use to change the world.

Nelson Mandela

With the high cost of post-secondary education, most young Canadians need help to finance their education past high school. And these young Canadians usually look to their parents for this financial assistance.

If you are saving for your children's education, consider setting up a Registered Education Savings Plan (RESP). This federal government program allows savings for education to grow tax free until the beneficiary, the student named in the RESP, enrolls in post-secondary education and money is withdrawn from the RESP. The withdrawn money is considered the student's income and hence any income tax owing is paid at the student's tax rate. A tax break on RESP income may be available to students who receive scholarships and bursaries.

There is no annual maximum RESP contribution and the lifetime maximum is $50,000 per child.

An RESP is a particularly worthwhile investment due to the federal government's Basic Canada Education Savings Grant (CESG). On application, each beneficiary receives a grant of $500 on an annual RESP contribution of $2,500 or more. The lifetime maximum CESG is $7,200 per beneficiary. The maximum

An RESP is a particularly worthwhile investment due to the federal government's Basic Canada Education Savings Grant (CESG).

CESG for any one year is $1,000, which allows a contributor to receive a grant for any unused grant room due to contributions below the maximum in previous years.

Additional government grants in the form of a $500 Canada Learning Bond may be available to students if a family is entitled to the National Child Benefit Supplement. Those who reside in Alberta can take advantage of a $500 Alberta Centennial Education Savings Grant.

There are many options for setting up an RESP and for investing the money in the account. Most banks and stockbrokers offer RESP accounts. Organizations called scholarship trusts whose only business is education savings plans, also offer RESPs. Be wary of the high enrollment fees charged by these businesses.

As with other investments, you need to shop very carefully and think for yourself before choosing an RESP plan. Read all the fine print in the account application package. Pay particular attention to what fees are charged and your options for collapsing the RESP if your child does not attend a qualifying educational institution.

To set up an RESP account, you need the Social Insurance Number for the child who is the beneficiary of the plan.

Choices for investing RESP money range from Guaranteed Investment Certificates (GIC) to mutual funds to self-directed plans with a choice of stocks, bonds, GICs or mutual funds. RESPs should be invested in a manner that ensures the money is available when the student needs it. For example, for the first years of the plan, you could invest based on a balanced asset allocation, and then migrate to a more conservative income asset allocation about 5 years before the student needs the money. See Chapter 10 for more discussion on asset allocation and risk.

23

Insurance, Annuities and Investing

...purchasing insurance is implicitly a hedge, not an investment.

Moshe Milevsky and Aron Gottesman, *Insurance Logic*

Insurance that Protects Financial Assets

There are insurance programs in place in Canada to protect certain types of financial assets if a financial organization goes bankrupt. You can reduce your investing risk by choosing investments covered by one of the insurance programs described below.

Money Deposited in Banks

The Canada Deposit Insurance Corporation (CDIC), a federal Crown corporation, automatically insures eligible deposits and reimburses depositors if a member institution fails. Virtually all the banks in Canada are members.

The insurance is limited to Canadian currency deposits payable in Canada, so accounts in U.S. dollars and other foreign currencies are not covered. It insures savings and chequing accounts, term deposits of 5 years or less, money orders and drafts, debentures issued by loan companies, certified drafts and cheques and traveller's cheques issued by member companies. There is a limit of $100,000 per eligible account.

The CDIC web site, <www.cdic.ca>, has a complete list of member institutions and more details on the insurance coverage.

Money Deposited in Credit Unions

Each province has it own organization and, hence, its own insurance scheme to protect credit union deposits. In some cases, the coverage is better than the CDIC. For example, the Manitoba Credit Union Deposit Guarantee Corporation coverage includes foreign currency deposits and term deposits longer than 5 years.

The Financial Consumer Agency of Canada web site, <www.fcac-acfc.gc.ca>, includes a list of provincial credit union insurance organizations and a web link for each.

Investments Held by Investment Dealers

Investment dealers in Canada have set up the Canadian Investor Protection Fund, an insurance fund that covers financial losses by customers of a member company that becomes bankrupt.

The fund provides up to $1 million coverage for a customer's general account and up to $1 million for total losses in other accounts, such as RRSPs, cash accounts, etc. See <www.cipf.ca> for a list of members and more details on the insurance coverage.

Universal Life Insurance and Tax-Free Investing

Personally, I am not a fan of universal life insurance because I believe most people are able to buy the coverage they need at a lower cost by purchasing term insurance. However, in certain personal situations, there may be merit in buying universal life insurance due to the tax benefits it provides.

Universal life insurance can be structured such that part of the premium goes into a savings fund that grows tax free. The policyholder decides how to invest this savings fund and is usually able to choose from a selection of Guaranteed Investment Certificates (GICs) and mutual funds. If you cancel the policy, you get back the money in the savings fund and pay tax on your net profits. On the death of the insured person, some universal life policies pay out the insurance amount plus the cash value of the savings fund tax free. So, beneficiaries of the policyholder's estate do not pay income taxes on the investment growth in the savings fund.

All of this comes at a cost. Insurance premiums on universal life are high, savings fund administrative expenses can be substantial and there is a significant financial penalty to get out of a universal life policy in the first 10 years.

If you plan to purchase life insurance anyway and will leave a substantial estate to your heirs, universal life insurance, with its savings fund option, may be suitable for you.

> Universal life insurance and annuities are complicated products with many options and constraints. Research policies thoroughly before buying.

The foregoing is a very simplified description of universal life insurance. It is a complicated product with many options and constraints. Research universal life insurance policies thoroughly and talk to a number of insurance agents before committing to this product.

Annuities

An annuity is an insurance contract. It involves investing a specific sum of money with an insurance company and, in return, receiving regular income payments for a specified time period. Insurance companies offer many variations of this basic concept. Here are the main types on offer.

- A single life annuity makes payments as long as the annuitant (i.e., the person named in the annuity contract) is alive.
- A joint and last survivor life annuity makes payments as long as one of the two joint annuitants (such as a husband or wife) is alive. These annuities can be bought with or without a reduction in the payment when one of the two annuitants dies.
- A life annuity with a guaranteed payment period makes payments for a specified minimum length of time or number of payments whether or not the annuitant(s) is/are alive.
- Term annuities pay out for a specified period of time.
- An accelerated annuity offers higher income payments for a person with a serious illness.
- An insured annuity combines an annuity with a life insurance policy. This ensures that money is left to your estate.

- A prescribed annuity has the potential to reduce your tax bill if bought with funds that are not drawn from a registered account such as an RRSP.
- Variable annuities provide non-guaranteed payments based on the performance of specific assets that are usually a portfolio of securities.

People without pensions may decide to purchase an annuity in order to have a guaranteed regular income. In fact, annuities are one of the options for collapsing an RRSP.

Annuity payments are a blend of return of capital (the money paid to the insurance company initially) and interest. Because no tax is paid on the capital being returned (you likely already paid tax on this money), there is less income tax owing compared to the same amount of income paid from a RRIF. These facts make it challenging to determine if an annuity is the best investment for your particular circumstances.

Annuities are complex contracts. Once purchased, they are irrevocable. You are committed to the terms of the contract.

If you are thinking of buying an annuity, do your homework. Get advice from financial advisors who can explain the pros and cons of the various options available for generating a regular income. Consult at least one advisor who is not in the business of selling annuities. Obtain quotes from a number of insurance agents. Make sure that the quotes include annuities offered by several different insurance companies. Compare the annuity payments you would receive to other options for a steady income stream, such as buying a 30-year government bond.

Above all, *Think for yourself*, before committing to an annuity.

24

Estate Planning and Investments

In this world nothing can be said to be certain, except death and taxes.

Benjamin Franklin

You likely have specific wishes regarding the fate of your worldly possessions after you die. Wishes like which child will inherit the family jewels? What should be done about the family cottage? How much money to bequeath to the local hospital?

To make sure these wishes are fulfilled, you need to have a will, a document that specifically details how your estate, that is, the personal possessions you leave, will be distributed. If you do not have a will, rules in the province where you live dictate how your estate will be disbursed.

To ensure that your wishes regarding your estate are respected, you need to do some estate planning and you need a will that is written in unambiguous, legally defensible language. I recommend that all investors seek assistance regarding estate planning and preparing their will from a lawyer who is knowledgeable in these areas.

> If you do not have a will, rules in the province where you live dictate how your estate will be disbursed.

Your will should include detailed provisions for the disposition of your investments. There are several investment related issues to consider when planning your estate and writing your will.

- Your estate will be executed as if all your property and investments were sold at your death. Capital gains taxes due on this "deemed disposition" could result in a large income tax bill that must be paid before any assets can be given to beneficiaries.
- Do you want all or some of your investments liquidated and the money distributed to beneficiaries?
- Do you want to leave certain stocks or other investments to certain people or a favourite charity?
- How will the family cottage be handled? There is likely to be a large amount of tax owing on the capital gain made on the property, even if the cottage isn't sold.
- Do you own enough U.S. assets to trigger U.S. estate tax?
- Does your will need provisions to manage the impact on your beneficiaries of receiving their inheritance? For example, should a grandchild's inheritance be placed in an investment trust that can only be accessed once he/she reaches the age of majority?
- Is the executor you have named capable of executing your wishes regarding disposition of your investments?
- Should your will specify that the executor retain professional assistance to handle disposition of your investments?
- Executing a will, especially one involving disposition of an investment portfolio, is a time consuming, complicated, bureaucratic process. Should a professional estate trustee be specified to execute your will?

The foregoing list is not exhaustive. Rather, it is designed to motivate you to review your wishes regarding the disposition of your estate and to take the necessary estate planning steps to ensure that these wishes will be respected after your death.

Part VII

Building and Maintaining Your Investment Portfolio

25

Creating an Investment Plan and Building an Investment Portfolio

*The time of maximum pessimism is the best time to buy
and the time of maximum optimism is the best time to sell.*

John Templeton

The investing journey begun in Chapter 1 is almost complete. Along the voyage, you've gained essential knowledge about investing. Your challenge now is to use this knowledge to write a personal investment plan and build a portfolio of successful investments. These critical steps for successful investing are the topic of this chapter.

I've included examples of investment portfolios for the various asset allocations discussed in Chapter 9. *Do not blindly follow these portfolios, they are merely examples for illustrative purposes.* Select investments for your own portfolio based on your individual needs using the tools outlined in this book. Remember universal investing rule number 1: Think for yourself.

In the portfolios on the following pages:

• equities means equities of developed markets; the stocks of companies based in Canada, U.S., Western Europe, Australia, New Zealand and Japan and

- emerging markets means stocks of companies based in other countries (India, China, Southeast Asia, Latin America, eastern Europe, Africa).

Creating an Investment Plan

When you are ready to prepare your investment plan, whether you are a do-it-yourself investor or you use a financial advisor, take sufficient time to focus exclusively on this task. Write a draft plan, take some time to reflect on your initial ideas, then revise the plan as needed.

While an investment plan needs to be tailored to individual circumstances, there are some elements common to all plans:

- the two fundamental steps of all investment plans; pay off debt first and pay yourself before you spend;
- your personal investing goals, short term and long term;
- desired timelines to achieve your goals;
- the rate of return you expect to achieve;
- the level of risk you are willing to assume. How large a drop in the value of your portfolio are you willing to accept?;
- the asset classes of investments you plan to buy;
- the target per cent range of each asset class and
- how you will determine the return rate of your portfolio.

Your investment plan is the roadmap to build your investment portfolio.

While you're in the planning mode, if you don't have an overall personal financial plan, spend the extra time to put one together. Such plans deal not only with investing, but also such things as your long-term financial goals, tax planning, retirement planning, and estate planning. I have personally found that the assistance of a professional financial planner to prepare an overall personal financial plan is a worthwhile investment.

Your investment plan is the roadmap to build your investment portfolio, the subject of the next sections.

Saving Money for Your First Portfolio

In order to construct your first investment portfolio, you need a big enough pot of money to be able to adequately diversify your investments. Thus, step one for any new investor is to save up this pot of money.

An easy way to start saving money regularly is to open a high interest savings account at a local bank. If your employer has a savings plan, this is a great way to save: the savings are automatically deducted from your pay and your employer may even kick in a contribution.

Start Up Portfolios

Once you've saved about $2,000, you can begin to build an investment portfolio by using mutual funds. For accounts of this size, the easiest way (and sometimes the only way given the high account minimums set by most financial advisors and stockbrokers) is to invest at a local bank or credit union branch. These branches offer basic financial advice. Available investments include Guaranteed Investment Certificates (GICs), Canada Savings Bonds (CSBs) and mutual funds. The low purchase minimum for the in-house brand of funds, usually $500, allows for reasonable diversification in small accounts. Minimums for further purchases of the same fund are usually lower. Many banks offer a regular fund purchase plan with automatic withdrawal from your bank account. Any dividends distributed by the fund are automatically reinvested in the fund without any purchase costs.

The two portfolios set out in Figure 25.1 are examples of balanced asset allocation portfolios based on bank brand mutual fund portfolios. These portfolios can be set up with approximately $2,000.

As an alternative, you can start building your portfolio by investing directly with an independent mutual fund company. However, most of these companies require initial investments of $5,000 or more.

Figure 25.1

Sample Start Up Balanced Portfolios

Asset Type & %		Sample Investments
Cash	5	ING Direct Savings Account
Bonds/GICs	45	CIBC Canadian Bond Fund
Bonds – Foreign	0	
Equities	50	CIBC Dividend Fund
		CIBC Global Equity Fund
Real Estate	0	
Emerging Markets	0	

Asset Type & %		Sample Investments
Cash	5	TD Canadian Money Market Fund
Bonds/GICs	45	TD Canadian Bond Index Fund
Bonds – Foreign	0	
Equities	50	TD Dividend Growth Fund
		TD U.S. Index Fund
		TD International Index Fund
Real Estate	0	
Emerging Markets	0	

Moderate Size Portfolios

As your investment portfolio grows, your investment choices expand and, with this, the potential for better investment returns.

With a portfolio of $25,000, investors can construct a diversified portfolio using Exchange-Traded Funds (ETFs) and the best of a wide selection of mutual funds. You need an account about this size to allow for adequate investment diversification, given that many of the better mutual funds have purchase minimums of $5,000 or more and ETFs are normally bought in lots of 100 shares.

To have access to this wider choice of investments, you may need to move beyond bank branch investing. So, once your portfolio approaches $25,000, start investigating other financial services options. Ideally, the financial service provider you choose should offer a broad choice of investments including stock trading and a good selection of mutual funds, not just their own house brand.

The table in Figure 25.2 shows an example of a balanced portfolio built for a $25,000 account using ETFs and mutual funds with good performance for their class. Note that different brands of mutual funds have been chosen. Generally, no one mutual fund company offers the best performing funds across all asset classes.

Figure 25.2
Model Balanced Portfolio, $25,000 Account

Asset Type & %		Sample Investments
Cash	5	ICIC Bank HiSave Savings Account
Bonds/GICs	40	Bissett Bond Fund
		iShares Real Return Bond Index Fund (XRB)
Bonds – Foreign	5	RBC Global Bond Fund
Equities	45	Scotia Canadian Dividend Fund
		iShares Canadian S&P 500 ETF (XSP)
		Mawer World Investment Fund
Real Estate	5	iShares Canadian REIT Sector ETF (XRE)
Emerging Markets	0	

Larger Portfolios

Once the equity component of your portfolio reaches about $50,000, you no longer need to rely exclusively on equity mutual funds. With this much money, you can purchase enough different stocks to build an adequately diversified portfolio. You may still want to own equity mutual funds and ETFs, particularly for investing in foreign stocks and small companies, but you now have the choice to directly own shares of companies.

The tables in Figure 25.3 set out examples of portfolios that can be built for larger investment accounts. They include investments for the five sample asset allocation portfolios described in Chapter 10, income, income focused, balanced, growth and aggressive growth.

Figure 25.3

Five Sample Asset Allocation Portfolios

Income Portfolio

Asset Type & %		Sample Investments
Cash	5	PC Financial Interest Plus Savings Account
Bonds/GICs	60	Guaranteed Investment Certificates (GIC) or bonds maturing in 1, 2, 3, 4 and 5 years
Bonds – Foreign	5	AGF Global Government Bond Fund (US$)
Equities	30	
Consumer, 6%		Corby's Distilleries (CDL.A) Shopper's Drug Mart (SC) Unilever (UN-NYSE)
Industrials, 6%		3M (MMM-NYSE) Johnson & Johnson (JNJ-NYSE) Thomson Corp (TOC)
Natural Resources, 6%		BHP Billeton (BHP-NYSE) Encana (ECA) Imperial Oil (IMO)
Utilities, 6%		Enbridge (ENB) Fortis (FTS) Telus (T)
Financials, 6%		Bank of Nova Scotia (BNS) Great West Life (GWL) Royal Bank (RB)
Real Estate	0	
Emerging Markets	0	

Income Focused Portfolio

Asset Type & %		Sample Investments
Cash & Equiv.	5	Altamira High-Interest CashPerformer Account
Bonds/GICs	50	iShares Canadian Bond Index Fund (XBB)
		iShares Real Return Bond Index Fund (XRB)
Bonds — Foreign	5	CI Global Bond Fund (US$)
Equities	35	
Consumer, 7%		Canada Bread (CBY)
		Rothman's (ROC)
		Walgreens (WAG-NYSE)
Industrials, 7%		Canadian National Railway (CNR)
		GE (GE-NYSE)
		Pfizer (PFE-NYSE)
Natural Resources, 7%		Potash (POT)
		Suncor Energy (SU)
		Teck-Cominco (TCK.B)
Utilities, 7%		Canadian Utilities (CU)
		Transcanada (TRP)
		Verizon Communications (VZ-NYSE)
Financials, 7%		Bank of Montreal (BMO)
		IGM Financial (IGM)
		Sun Life Financial (SLF)
Real Estate	5	Dynamic FocusPlus Real Estate Fund
Emerging Markets	0	

Balanced Portfolio

Asset Type & %		Sample Investments
Cash & Equiv.	5	Manulife Financial Investment Savings Account
Bonds/GICs	40	Philip, Hager & North Total Return Bond Fund
		iShares Real Return Bond Index Fund (XRB)
Bonds – Foreign	5	Vanguard Total Bond Market ETF (BND-AMEX)
Equities	45	
Consumer, 9%		Canadian Tire (CTC.A)
		Procter and Gamble (PG-NYSE)
		Tim Hortons (THI)
Industrials, 9%		Finning (FTT)
		Microsoft (MSFT-Q)
		SNC-Lavalin (SNC)
Natural Resources, 9%		Cameco (CCO)
		Petro-Canada (PCA)
		Shawcor (SCL.A)
Utilities, 9%		Fortis (FTS)
		Shaw Communications (SJR.B)
		Transalta Corp. (TA)
Financials, 9%		CIBC (CM)
		Manulife Financial (MFC)
		Power Financial (PWF)
Real Estate	5	H&R REIT (HR.UN)
		Riocan REIT (REI.UN)
Emerging Markets	0	

Growth Portfolio

Asset Type & %		Sample Investments
Cash & Equiv.	5	Money market fund at your financial institution Canada 90 day T bills
Bonds/GICs	20	iShares Canadian Bond Index Fund (XBB) iShares Real Return Bond Index Fund (XRB)
Bonds – Foreign	5	Templeton Global Bond Fund
Equities	60	
Consumer, 10%		Cryptologic (CRY) MacDonalds (MCD-NYSE) Saputo (SAP)
Industrials, 10%		Canadian Pacific Railway (CP) FedEx (FDX-NYSE) Nokia (NOK-NYSE)
Natural Resources, 10%		HudBay Minerals (HBM) Agrium (AGV) Suncor Energy (SU)
Utilities, 10%		China Mobile (CHL-NYSE) Cogeco Cable (CCA) El Paso (EP-NYSE)
Financials, 10%		National Bank (NA) Sun Life Financial (SLF) TD Bank (TD)
Small Company, 10%		CI American Small Companies Fund (US$) Saxon Small Cap Fund
Real Estate	5	Calloway REIT (CWT.UN) Melcor Developments (MRD)
Emerging Markets	5	AGF Emerging Markets Value Fund (US$)

Aggressive Growth Portfolio

Asset Type & %		Sample Investments
Cash & Equiv.	5	Canadian Tire High Interest Savings Account
		Canada 90 day T bills
Bonds/GICs	5	iShares Short Bond Index Fund (XSB)
		iShares Canadian Long Bond Index Fund (XLB)
Bonds – Foreign	5	Templeton Global Income Fund (GIM-NYSE)
Equities	70	
Consumer, 12%		Metro (MRU.A)
		Pepsico (PEP-NYSE)
		Royal Caribbean Cruises (RCL-NYSE)
Industrials, 12%		Stantec (STN)
		PPG Industries (PPG-NYSE)
		Research in Motion (RIM)
Natural Resources, 12%		Barrick Gold (ABX)
		Canadian Natural Resources (CNQ)
		West Fraser Timber (WFT)
Utilities, 12%		Atco (ACO.X)
		Manitoba Telecom (MBT)
		Transcanada (TRP)
Financials, 12%		Barclays Bank (BCS-NYSE)
		Canada Western Bank (CWB)
		Power Corp (POW)
Small companies, 10%		Steadyhand Small Cap Equity Fund
		Trimark Global Small Companies Fund (US$)
Real Estate	10	BPO Properties (BPP)
		Legacy Hotels REIT (LGY.UN)
Emerging Markets	5	Vanguard Emerging Markets ETF (VWO-AMEX)

The Lazy Investor Portfolio

Periodically, the investing media report on portfolios that have been concocted for the lazy investor. You may have heard about the couch potato portfolio, the two-minute portfolio and the easy-chair portfolio, all variations on this theme. These portfolios consist of fixed percentages of specific investments. The idea is to look at the portfolio just once a year and buy and sell as needed to revert to the original investment allocation.

Lazy investor portfolios are based on the premise that investors can make decent investment returns while spending minimal time ministering to their investments. Retrospective studies of the performance of such portfolios suggest that this may be true.

The sample moderate risk portfolio in Figure 25.4 follows the lazy investor tradition. It is built using ETFs. For those who save and invest regularly (e.g., a fixed amount from every pay cheque), a similar portfolio can be constructed with equivalent index mutual funds to escape the transaction costs of ETFs.

Figure 25.4

Lazy Investor Portfolio

Asset Type & %		Sample Investments
Cash	5	Canadian T-Bill Fund
Bonds/GICs	35	iShares Canadian Bond Index Fund (XBB)
		iShares Real Return Bond Index Fund (XRB)
Equities	60	25% iShares Canadian Dividend (XDV)
		25% Claymore U.S. Fundamental Index ETF (CLU)
		10 % iShares Canadian MSCI EAFE (XIN)

26

Ongoing Management of Your Investments

Risk comes from not knowing what you're doing.

Warren Buffett

So, you've made a plan, you've established investing goals and set up an investment portfolio. That's the first inning of investing. There are more innings to this game. In this chapter, I'll discuss what it takes to stay in the investment game.

Continuing to Save and Invest

To reach your investment goals after setting up a portfolio, you need to continue to save, invest these savings and reinvest the dividends you receive from your investments.

Some financial services firms make it easy to save and invest by offering automatic savings plans. Banks and credit unions offer automatic monthly transfer of fixed sums from your regular account to your investing account. Some plans provide monthly automatic withdrawal of a fixed amount from your chequing account and investment of the money in mutual funds you have specified.

If your financial services provider offers a dividend reinvestment plan, consider signing up. The plan automatically reinvests the dividends you receive in additional shares or units at low or no cost to you. (See Synthetic Dividend Reinvestment Plans in Chapter 7 for more details.)

Some financial service providers such as eTrade will automatically move cash in your account to a money market fund.

If you do not participate in the aforementioned automated plans, do regularly move any spare cash in your investing account into a short-term savings vehicle such as a money market fund. This keeps every invested dollar working for you. Once your cash holding is sufficiently large, use the money to purchase an investment.

Recordkeeping

Successful investors keep records to:

- know what they own,
- monitor their investments,
- track investment returns and
- satisfy legal requirements such as tax owing on capital gains.

Investing recordkeeping doesn't need to be onerous, but it should be routine. Here are the basics.

- Establish a fixed location for your records, such as a binder or file folders in a filing cabinet.
- Decide on a filing system structure. I file by chronological order; other systems such as an alphabetical system by investment name may better suit your needs.
- File all account statements (usually received monthly or quarterly) from your financial services provider.
- File all the buy/sell notices sent from your financial services provider.
- Set up a spreadsheet to track the timing and the reasons for your investment purchases and sales. Make sure you record the acquisition cost and sale price of any investment that could generate capital gains. Knowing this figure is crucial to calculate any capital gains (or losses) created when the investment is sold. The Stock Recordkeeping Form in Figure 26.1 is an example of how this might be done.
- At the beginning of the year set up a new file for the year and store the previous year's statements and buy/sell notices. These records should be kept for 7 years for income tax purposes.

Recordkeeping needn't be time consuming. Make it a routine part of investing and you'll have fewer headaches at tax time and be able to easily track your progress in meeting your investment goals.

Monitoring Your Investments

You don't need to check your investments every day or even every week.

You don't need to check your investments every day or even every week. You do need to review any notices and investment statements from your financial services provider to ensure they are correct and to identify any actions you must take. For example, you may need to reinvest the money from a bond that has come due. Or, you may need to decide whether or not to accept a takeover offer for the shares of a company you own.

Monitoring your investments also includes scanning any articles/investing reports you see regarding an investment you own to decide if the information provided necessitates any action regarding your investments.

Periodic Review and Update of Your Investment Plan

You know if you are winning or losing the investment game by periodically measuring progress toward your investment goals and adjusting the goals and your investments as needed. I recommend that you complete a short review of your investment progress after the end of each calendar quarter (April, July, October) and undertake a detailed review of your investment plan after the end of the calendar year (January). Wait until you receive your investment account statement(s) to begin these reviews.

Quarterly Review of Investments

Your quarterly review should usually include these actions.

- Discuss your investment portfolio with your financial advisor.
- Review the performance of individual investments and scan the quarterly earnings report of any companies you own. Sell any investments that no longer meet your investing criteria.

- Identify any asset classes that vary significantly from their target ranges.
- Identify potential investments, particularly in asset classes where your investments are below your target allocation. Put these on your buy list for possible purchase.
- Invest any cash where needed to adjust your asset mix toward your target ranges.
- Establish a time frame to buy or sell investments as needed to achieve your target asset allocation.

Annual Investment Plan Review

Your annual review should be a thorough evaluation of your investment plan and investments and should cover the areas noted.

- Review the performance of your overall portfolio.
- Review what you have bought and sold over the previous year and take note of the reasons for your investment successes and failures.
- Review your investment goals, determine if they still meet your needs and revise your goals as necessary. This is the time to consider changes to your current asset allocation.
- Review the performance of individual investments and sell any investments that no longer meet your investing criteria.
- Identify asset classes outside of their target allocation.
- Identify potential investments. Put these on your possible buy list.
- Invest any cash where needed to adjust your asset mix toward your target ranges.
- Establish a time frame to buy or sell investments as needed to achieve your target asset allocation.

Wrapping Up – It's Your Money and Your Life

My goal in writing this book was to provide you, the individual Canadian investor, with the straight goods on investing your money. If you have stayed with me throughout these pages, I believe you are now equipped to make informed decisions about how to reach your investment goals. I sincerely hope that this book provokes all who read it to take charge of their investments.

When making investment decisions, always remember the five universal rules of investing.

1. Think for yourself.
2. Know yourself.
3. Manage your risk.
4. Be patient.
5. Be decisive.

Above all, don't forget that life is for living and successful investing provides a means to live your life the way you want.

Figure 26.1
Stock Recordkeeping Form

Portfolio Record		Account Name		Regular Investment				Disposition	Today's Date		31-Oct-07
Stock or Asset	Trans-action Date	Transaction Type and Reason	Purchase Asset Cost including Fees	Total $ Invested to Date	# Shares Acquired	Total # Shares Held	Current Adjusted Cost Base per share	# Shares Sold	Proceeds	Cost of Shares Sold	Capital Gain or Loss
stock X	8-Dec-06	Purchase New product released	$3,000.00	$3,000.00	100	100	$30.00				
stock X	12-Dec-06	Purchase General market correction	$3,200.00	$6,200.00	100	200	$31.00				
stock X	8-Oct-07	Sale Revenue outlook poor					$31.00	100	$3,600.00	$3,100.00	$500.00

Index

No Hype

The Straight Goods on Investing Your Money

by Gail Bebee

Is there someone you know who could benefit from reading *No Hype—The Straight Goods on Investing Your Money*? It makes a great gift for Canadians looking for clear, unbiased information on investing.

To order additional copies:
1. Visit us online at www.nohypeinvesting.com or,
2. Complete this form and mail it with your cheque to:
   The Ganneth Company
   17 Blithfield Avenue
   Toronto, Ontario
   M2K 1X9

Please send me _____ copies of

No Hype–*The Straight Goods on Investing Your Money*

at $28.00 each (includes GST and shipping)
Enclosed is my cheque payable to **The Ganneth Company**
in the amount of $_____ (Cdn).

☐ Check here for an autographed copy. For a personal dedication, please enclose desired wording.

Full Name: _____

Address: _____

City: _____ Province: _____ Postal code: _____

Tel. or Email: _____
                                               (to confirm shipment)
☐ Yes, keep me updated on No Hype news and special offers.

Please allow 1 to 2 weeks for delivery.

For orders of 10 or more books, we offer attractive discounts.
The author is available for speaking engagements.
Please contact us for details.
Web site: **www.nohypeinvesting.com**
Email: **info@nohypeinvesting.com**